This book is brilliant. The closest a
the question 'how do I lead chang
Jeremy Small – CEO ar

We are amidst a sea change in the legal sector. Global pressures, digitisation, and a departure from traditional billing and resourcing mean lawyers and those who lead them need to adapt fast. This book, full of real-life examples and practical tips, shows us how. Scarr's CARE model demonstrates how to create an optimum environment for growth at every level. Through connecting with a deeper organizational purpose and relating meaningfully with those around us, we can all become more conscious lawyers and leaders.

Justin D'Agostino – Chief Executive Officer and Partner,
Herbert Smith Freehills LLP

This is a great reminder that times of change present opportunities, and that our teams, more than ever, need leadership rather than management. *The Conscious Lawyer* is full of nuggets on how to maximize the opportunities in front of us and ensure that our teams are fully motivated and engaged in the journey.

Tim Casben – Managing Partner UAE, Gowling WLG

This book is a game-changer. It caused me to look inside myself to uncover my purpose, ask myself the honest question of what kind of legacy I want to have as a leader and remind myself that it's okay to be human and to show humility, empathy and compassion.

Catherine Workman – Partner and Head of Middle East,
Pinsent Masons

The Conscious Lawyer makes us think about our approach to leadership and the impact we have in both the legal and business world. It affirms the importance of being human, having empathy and allowing the heart to play an essential role in our decision making. A must read for senior leaders and aspiring leaders of the future!

**Rania Tadros – Managing Partner,
Stephenson Harwood Middle East**

In *The Conscious Lawyer*, Kiran Scarr shares a unique insider's view of the legal profession. Her vision of the profession's future is both compelling and timely, as we take stock of shifting generational preferences and the tough lessons dealt out by the Covid-19 pandemic. A must-read for those in leadership roles within the legal sector or, indeed, any industry sector.

Patrick Earl – Chief Operating Officer, Al Tamimi & Co

Law firms are coming under increased pressure from global economic challenges, technological disruption and generational shifts in the workplace. We are in new frontiers of growth and purpose where measures of success expand beyond financial indicators. *The Conscious Lawyer* tells us how we need to change as leaders to respond to this urgent call to action. An essential read for any professional ready to lead through change in the legal sector.

**Nick Roberts – Head of Legal Delivery and Innovation,
Clyde & Co**

For centuries, we have lived in a world where a leader's status has eclipsed the needs of those they lead. Ongoing geopolitical turmoil, persistent inflation and economic uncertainty are testing a leader's ability to navigate uncertainty. In this new era of purpose, trust and inclusion, new leadership is required. Kiran Scarr takes us on a journey from our own limitations to choosing greater impact. This book will guide you to become an authentic change agent and help you create the positive impact that is so needed in this world.

Iris Van der Veken – Executive Director and Secretary General, Watch & Jewellery Initiative 2030

Kiran's 'CARE' model is a simple guide in how to step up to a higher standard of responsibility for people and performance in the businesses we serve. A must for every leader facing disruption, challenge and uncertainty in today's globalised economy.

Sophie Moloney – Chief Executive Officer, Sky New Zealand

With *The Conscious Lawyer*, Kiran Scarr sets a vision for the future of the profession: a vision of leadership, humanity and courage. A vision in which values and impact drive results. And one in which lawyers can take down their mask to build a stronger brand. The book is essential reading for lawyers and all those thinking of becoming one, providing a framework for a better future.

Mark Beer OBE – Professor of AI and the Law, Shanghai University of Political Science and Law

This book is aimed not just at legal practitioners but us all. Change is all around us as new technologies emerge, as existing business models are upended and as the war for talent becomes even more fierce. Doing what we always did, and expecting the same outcomes is not enough. Change we must, and this book gives us ample food for thought and reflection on how to do just that. An excellent read.

Gautam Sashittal – Chief Executive Officer, King Abdullah Financial District

Kiran understands the urgent need for a change in mindset and approach among legal leaders. This book provides a range of deeply-researched and thoughtful observations on leadership, and will be of use to any lawyer interested in developing themselves, the team they lead and the institutions they serve.

Andrew Cooke – General Counsel, TravelPerk

This is a must-read for any lawyers looking to distinguish themselves as a leading in-house counsel, or for those looking to fully understand the needs of an in-house counsel as their client. *The Conscious Lawyer* is full of wonderful insights and thought-provoking perspectives on the current failing in the legal sector, and the behavioral change needed to be a great leader.

Justin Dowding – Head of Legal Middle East, Africa, Turkey and Pakistan, TikTok

This book is a journey into redefining values, purpose, and success. Kiran gracefully takes us on the courageous path to challenging the myths that pervade our profession to shift our focus from doing high-performance to being a people enabler. An essential read for those who want to know how to embrace change.

Filippo Cossalter – Head of Legal, Johnson & Johnson Emerging Markets and Italy and member of the board of directors, Association of Corporate Counsel Middle East and North Africa

The Conscious Lawyer fully captures the raw challenges facing lawyers in private practice and in-house roles today. Packed with practical solutions to everyday leadership problems, it gives a clear roadmap in how to drive our transformation journey from controlling results to focusing attention on people. Read this book if you want to unleash your potential to be an influential leader of your team and your business.

Dr Yasser Aboismail – General Counsel, Schindler

A unique perspective on how to change mindset and behaviour in high performing teams. What it reveals about lawyers' ability to change how they lead themselves and their businesses is both exciting and hopeful.

Mark Hultum – Regional Head of Legal, International Bank

With *The Conscious Lawyer*, Kiran Scarr has taken leadership in the legal sector to a new, inspiring level. If you want to lead change in your law firm or legal function, you must read this book.

Allison Hosking – Director of NewLaw, PwC Legal Middle East

Digital transformation for any law firm or corporate legal department is a long journey that goes far beyond purchasing the right legal technology solution. It requires lawyers to take a holistic approach to change, prioritising how to lead change within their organizations. *The Conscious Lawyer* guides us on how to do just that. It is an essential read for any lawyer ready to lead through radical change in the legal sector.

Ibrahim Abdel Rehim – Regional Head Middle East Africa Russia/CIS and India, Thomson Reuters

THE ᒿONSCIOUS LAWYER

Courageous leadership for high-performing professionals

KIRAN SCARR

First published in Great Britain by Practical Inspiration Publishing, 2023

ISBN   9781788604437   (print)
        9781788604451   (epub)
        9781788604444   (mobi)

Want to bulk-buy copies of this book for your team and colleagues? We can customize the content and co-brand *The Conscious Lawyer* to suit your business's needs.

Please email info@practicalinspiration.com for more details.

To Dad, who showed me, from the beginning,
humility in a life of service.

Contents

Preface

Where it began

It is 14 February 2018, a cold, crisp day at the top of a ski mountain in the French Alps. I look up at the cloudless sky and smile; it is my first day on a long-overdue holiday. I kick off, feeling the thrill of my first descent through the powdery snow. I stop mid-slope to allow a group of small children to zigzag past me. I am observing how freely they move when, suddenly, my legs are thrown above my head and I am falling through the air. Silence engulfs me except for one sound, a twig snapping. But it is not a twig that has snapped. It is the anterior cruciate ligament in my right knee. What I just heard was the sound of a clean tear.

I have been hit from behind by a skier. What follows is an evacuation by stretcher to the local emergency room, where a doctor comes to examine me. 'Where does it hurt?' she asks. I look at her straight. 'I have an extremely high pain threshold', I respond. The doctor is confused. She asks me again, 'Where do you feel the pain?' I lie there in silence. Tears start to well in my eyes. 'Don't cry,' she says, 'I can help you.' I close my eyes, hurriedly wiping the tears as they surface. I am overcome with shame. At that moment, lying broken on a hospital bed, I realize I cannot admit to being in pain.

That accident started a rehabilitative journey for not only my knee but also my head, my heart, and my soul. My post-operation recovery became an exploration into my relationship with pain, my inability to ask for help, and my unwillingness to accept defeat. Through this challenging process of discovery, I started to explore my definition of success and fulfilment. Not knowing where this journey would take me, I was simply compelled to go on. What I did not know then was that I had started on the path of transformation to being a conscious lawyer.

Why it is time to change

Lawyers are under unprecedented levels of pressure and stress from global challenges, technological disruption, and generational shifts in the workplace. We must deliver more with less. We must create new business models, innovative solutions to meet client demands, and better talent retention capabilities.

As high-performing professionals, we define success through delivering exceptional results. The more we achieve, the deeper we dig in and push for even better results to maintain our positions at the top. The financial rewards are great, but the cost to our personal fulfilment is high.

We have never needed leadership transformation as much as we do right now. Leaders of law firms and legal functions are being called on to be creative and innovative leaders of change. But in the absence of knowing *how* to change, we simply soldier on, unconsciously surrendering to diminishing fulfilment in life and work. But there is a path ahead that we can take. We can choose to be conscious lawyers.

What it means to be a conscious lawyer

When we choose to lead consciously, we are choosing a journey that teaches us to shift attention from doing high performance to being leaders in our own lives. It means purposefully stepping into a higher level of responsibility and integrity to lead through disruptive change in the legal sector.

Conscious lawyers shift focus from producing high performance results to unleashing untapped potential in people. This requires a courageous leap to valuing learning over performance and process over results. We become growth leaders of change by building new leadership skills focused on transforming how we deliver success, prioritizing vision and values, purpose over profits, and positive impact on people.

Conscious lawyers engage people in the higher purpose of transforming legal operations, resourcing, and service delivery. And in doing so, they empower the change leaders of tomorrow to fulfil their highest potential in delivering the future of law.

I have written *The Conscious Lawyer* to help you discover a more meaningful way of leading high-performing teams through change in the legal sector.

My approach

In Chapter 3, I outline my CARE model – a four-leap process that takes you through the shift from leading high performance results to unleashing untapped potential in people. In describing the model, I have drawn heavily on my own experience as an international lawyer, general counsel, and law firm chief operating officer (COO). I have also leaned on my experience as an executive coach helping leaders of law firms and legal functions transform how they lead themselves and others through change. There are some points that I must clarify.

First, my case studies, examples, and stories are a combination of facts and circumstances that are grounded in truth but have been adapted and developed to protect the confidentiality of the people involved. I identify individuals using random initials rather than actual names. In some cases, I have merged events or individuals where they relate to similar themes or points. As a result, there are cases where I have erred on the side of sanctity of trust over sanctity of truth.

Second, I have tried to be gender agnostic in my case studies, examples, and stories. I am a passionate believer that radical change in the legal sector will come with greater diversity at board level in law firms and corporates, particularly through the promotion of women. However, I do not believe that the skills required to lead law firms and corporate legal functions are defined according to gender, race, religion, creed, or any other factor that may differentiate us. We all must evolve our leadership skill sets to create meaningful change for the people we serve. And we are all capable of change; it is simply a choice.

Finally, I wrote *The Conscious Lawyer* for lawyers and non-lawyer professionals working in the legal sector, because my passion lies in helping others advance the future of law. However, the learnings I share relate to issues affecting people in any sector facing disruption or global challenge. I hope the learnings in this book will give them food for thought too.

My path to being a conscious lawyer continues today, as it has for many days, months, and years. With each day comes greater learning. With each step forward, I come closer to fulfilling a deeper purpose in my life and work.

As we connect to our own consciousness,
We give others permission to connect to their
consciousness too,
So that we
Unlock greater meaning in our work,
Serve people in our lives, and
Have greater impact on this earth.

Chapter 1
Doing high performance

The problem with being a high-performing professional is that it can be rewarding and punishing in equal measure. The aspects of the job that provide us with wealth, power, and status also rob us of our self-worth. The more we do, the less we feel. It's time to change.

How we are taught to behave

When I look back at the 15 plus years I spent as a private practice lawyer, the word that consistently comes to mind is 'striving'. No amount of effort was ever enough. The primary measures of my performance were quantity and quality of input. Because of this, I poured the contents of my soul into being smarter, quicker, and keener than those around me. In the constant pursuit of perfection, I did not have time or space to connect to the bigger picture.

So focused was I on the glimpse of partnership at the end of a long, dark, and winding tunnel, there was no room for reflection, reality checks, or connection to me. The more machine-like I operated, the more seamless my delivery became. As the cogs continued to turn at increasing personal cost, I dug deeper into my reserves and submerged any doubts as to whether I would get there. It was all about results

– being on the best deals, delivering the strongest outcomes and fighting for the next opportunity – to prove my strength and hunger.

It strikes me now how the terminology used in the law firms where I worked reflected how we were expected to behave. Partners would refer to junior associates as 'troops'. Litigators had 'war rooms' and would talk in terms of 'crushing opponents', as if we had been posted to an eternal battlefield. In conversations with my peers now, we share stories of how it felt to be a young associate moving up the ranks of private practice. How we did not raise concerns or grievances in fear of being seen as weak or not a team player. And we talk about the impact this had on how we learnt to behave. For many of us, over time, our armour simply toughened and our resilience hardened. We soldiered on.

Does any of this resonate with you? Do you treat every challenge as a competition to be the best? In the face of challenge or obstacle, do you lean in and hustle your way through until you get what you want? How did you learn to behave? Certainly, in my case, I majored in the military approach to high performance. I would issue orders at will, expect loyalty and excellence from everyone, and demand results that met the highest of standards. People showed appreciation for my command and authority, my willingness to roll up my sleeves, and my ability to absorb and withstand the highest of pressures. My team showed respect for the flair I had for transforming stress into power.

The source of my power came from my ability to deliver exceptional results. In the context of Maxwell's (2013) five levels of leadership (refer to Table 1.1), I was operating squarely at Level 3 (production). The Level 3 leader gains credibility and influence not only because of their ability and competency but also because of their track record of success – the quantity and quality of work delivered. They are the quintessential 'high performer' with a reputation for tackling tough problems, solving the most complex of issues, and taking other people to a higher standard of effectiveness.

Table 1.1 John C. Maxwell's five levels of leadership as they relate to positions in the legal sector

Level		Description	Legal position
1	Position	Focus on *rights* Rely on position, systems, and policies to influence	Graduate, trainee
2	Permission	Focus on *relationships* Rely on building influence through team cohesion and being liked	Junior associate, legal counsel
3	Production	Focus on *results* Build credibility and influence through a track record of high performance results	Senior associate, senior counsel
4	People development	Focus on *unleashing potential in others* Build impact through creating the optimum environment for high potentials to become Level 4 leaders of the future	Partner, general counsel, head of legal
5	Pinnacle	Focus on *legacy* Build impact beyond the industry through philanthropy, pioneering, and innovation	Head of a society, foundation, or trust

Source: adapted from Maxwell (2013)

By upholding the traditional focus on financial results, Level 3 leaders can deploy resources and directly control achievement of goals and targets with maximized efficiency and effectiveness. Teams become high performing under this leadership approach because it gets the desired results – that is, specific, short-term business objectives are met. Success flows from this: leaders are recognized in their fields, attract awards for their deals, and are financially rewarded for their efforts. By making financial performance requirements the primary focus, they come to be relied on for exceptional results and profits year on year.

How we are measured

Law firms and corporates love performance criteria that measure people by revenues, profits per equity partner, cost savings, billable hours, and other financial indicators. When the primary success criterion by which we are measured is financial return from our efforts, our choices align with the most direct route to this destination. We are judged not on how we behave, but on what we deliver, so we shift our focus to demonstrating solutions and results, at whatever cost.

During my career, I spent some time observing the behaviour and interactions of a team of equity partners in an exceptionally high-performing international law practice. Table 1.2 describes what it looked like from where I was sitting.

Table 1.2 What high performance looks like in an international law practice

Pursuit	Behaviour of equity partners	Behaviour of lawyers
Clients	Act as a lone wolf	Strive to be chosen as the partners' pack leader
Management responsibilities	Vye for greater control for financial gain/safe harbour rather than personal and professional learning	Manage relationships for greater control of resources and, therefore, results
Win new work	Compete with partners internally for file opening status	Compete with team members for matter management status
Recognition	Constantly seek recognition for what was achieved	Constantly indulge in self-promotion
Physical presence	Be present in the office unnecessarily	Be present in the office to be seen
Meeting presence	Talk too much	Please too much
Networks	Optimize networks according to who they know	Optimize networks according to who they meet
Gravitas	Occupy bigger offices in better locations, take better car park spaces, talk about holiday homes in impressive locations	Wear expensive suits and watches, display car keys, tell exaggerated stories

In truth, at the time, I accepted these indicators at face value as the measures of success. In hindsight, I realize they translate into toxic workplace behaviour (this is discussed in greater detail in Chapter 12). In the context of my experience of people's behaviour in law firms, the impact of this environment was that we were measured not by our potential capacity for future success, but by our ability to deliver in the now. This meant that my decisions about what deals to work on were principally political, based on which partners I wanted to align with and for what specific purpose, rather than on long-term opportunity or potential for learning. I would grab every chance of new work from the partner who could advance my career quickest. As my success grew, I drew greater satisfaction from my results.

How high performers perceive themselves

I liked being a high performer; it was serving me very well. I had a strong team of lawyers who consistently sought to work with me. I felt pride in what I was able to consistently deliver. I would take command of what needed to be done, and I could make things happen. My instructions were always clear, concise, and results orientated. I was straightforward and conscious of time and time wasters. I was also very deliberate, thorough, and logical. My approach was systematic and disciplined. I remained calm and level-headed even in the throes of crisis or deadline.

It was robotic, in truth. Efficient, dependable, reliable. I liked it that way. It meant I had control. By reducing scope for uncertainty, delay, or complication, I could increase the likelihood of goal achievement on time and in budget. And I was sure my team loved it too. They knew what was expected of them and how high the bar was set in respect of quantity and quality of effort. I was always clear and exact in my feedback to them. I would not sugarcoat the negative, strong in my view that they would appreciate the openness and honesty of where they fell short of my high expectations. How else would they learn? And in appreciation of what we had achieved, I always ensured we celebrated a win or the closing of a deal. I was leading high performance and the results made me look and feel good; my ego shone bright.

The power gap

What I did not appreciate at the time when I was leading high performance was the cost of this endless execution. There may have been big wins, big deals, big results, but there was not much humanity. There was little space for what makes us human: vulnerability, humility, self-awareness, creativity. There was little acknowledgement of what I was experiencing in my daily life: detachment, desensitization, diminution of self-worth. Work had become an addiction; I was focusing on the next fix of a deal rather than facing the reality of the experience of a life I had created for myself.

When I donned my high-performance armour, I felt at my most powerful. On the fleeting occasions I stepped out of this armour – at home in private, sometimes with friends – it felt uncomfortable, uneasy, alien. I preferred to stay in character, knowing that the self I created would be perceived better than the version that lay beneath. High performance had created a power gap within me. On the surface, I was strong, solid, reflective of success. I had created an image for myself, and in time, I felt compelled to demonstrate that I was living up to this image. Rather than sit in the reality of how it felt to be vulnerable, in need of care and support, the impression of myself as a strong and powerful leader started to drive my choices and decisions in life. Work was my utmost priority, to be maintained above all. Demands became what I 'should' do instead of what I wanted to do. These choices overtook my reason and my conscience. Faced with a choice between a hard or an easy path, I would always choose the hard one. Because the hard path would make me stronger, more resilient, and worthy of the version of me I was living up to.

I feel I share this experience with many others in the legal profession. When I scroll through LinkedIn posts – the platform of choice for lawyers, particularly in the Middle East – I see so many high performers keen to project their brands in the face of competition. We each have created a version of ourselves that we are keen to live up to. We summarize this brand, unapologetically, as a tagline beneath our names – 'multi-award-winning litigator, problem-solver, disrupter', for example. And once we have stepped into this arena of self-promotion, we start to make choices that feed that reputation. We pursue keynote speaking roles and award nominations, attend countless events and networking opportunities, and celebrate successes as often as they arise. This is good provided it is in service of who we are. This is not good if it is feeding our ego-selves.

A coaching client, SP, came to me at a time when she was pushing for equity partnership and things were not going to plan. When I sat with SP at our first session, she cast her eyes downwards into the coffee cup she was holding and said: 'I do not know how this has happened. I just cannot believe my team would say these things about me. I don't even recognize who this person is they are describing.' We were going through the feedback she had received from a recent 360 review, which had resulted in SP being assigned behavioural coaching in lieu of promotion to equity. The review comments were tough to digest:

- 'I want to work with her, but she's relentless in her expectations of what I can do.'
- 'She's tough, and sometimes I wonder whether she even likes me.'
- 'She can be harsh and overly critical. It's as if she doesn't trust me anymore.'

SP pored over the words, searching for clues as to who said what and what incident they may have been referring to, as if this would hold the answers she craved. I took the paper from her hands, put it to one side, and asked, 'What do you want to do to change this?'

SP was stuck at Level 3 leadership (production), and it had simply stopped serving her. Whilst it was producing high performance results, the cost to SP and her team was too great. The pressures of billable hours, financial targets, and bringing in the next deal were taking their toll on her behaviour. SP's operating mode had become choosing the quickest, most efficient route to achieving desired results, regardless of the impact on other people. In the process, she had lost connection to who she is.

Being a conscious lawyer

The journey that SP and many of us must take when we reach senior positions in the legal sector is to elevate ourselves to Level 4 leadership (people development). This requires a conscious shift of focus from leading results to leading people. When we shift our focus from results to people, our attention is on the impact we have on people – more specifically, how we make them feel. In this enhanced field of vision, we acknowledge that our primary responsibility as leaders is to produce leaders of the future. Our role becomes less about directly delivering results and more about stepping back to create the optimum environment for our high-potential team members to become Level 4 leaders themselves.

When I look back at my days of leading high-performance team members through 'production' rather than 'people development', I realize that I misunderstood their motivations for being there. They delivered high performance results not because they wanted to; they delivered because they needed to. They did not consciously choose; they subconsciously surrendered. When I reflect on leading through people development, it feels radically different. When I finally stepped back to choose a new way of being a leader, I shifted my attention to the space I had created between me and the people around me. In that space lay the optimum environment for high performance: a culture of engaged and empowered people who are motivated to be inclusive, collaborative, creative, innovative, and courageous. My role was to work with each of them individually to enable them to operate at their highest level of contribution. I had to see them as wholly capable and resourceful, with potential that is limitless. I had to act as their guide, steward, coach, and mentor. I had to support them, recognize their efforts and successes, praise their progress and learning, and encourage them to overcome challenges and push through discomfort into growth.

I developed this approach during my years as a general counsel, and over time, as I increasingly focused my attention towards people, it released a desire in me to rehumanize. For so long I had relied solely on my head to operate the controls for making choices and taking actions. Slowly, I learnt that there was a much more reliable source of decision-making – my heart. As I started to trust myself to show compassion, vulnerability, empathy, and humour again, I discovered a much higher standard of care, responsibility, and power. I stepped into being a conscious lawyer.

Conscious lawyers are courageous enough to shift their attention from producing high performance to developing people. They embrace their humanness and show humility, empathy, and compassion. They are purpose driven, which means they prioritize sustainable outcomes over immediate profits. They are values based, aligning their decision-making with their organizational and personal values. They see change as a process, not a destination, so focus on transforming their impact on how people experience work. Their growth mindset means they focus on unleashing the unlimited potential of people to exceed their own expectations of what they can do and learn. And in doing so, they give the people around them permission to contribute at their highest level.

When we choose to lead consciously, we are choosing an infinite journey that teaches us a fundamental shift in attention from doing high performance to being a leader. It means purposefully stepping into a higher level of responsibility and integrity (Mackey, McIntosh, and Phipps, 2020, p. xv). This marks a fundamental change in how we behave every day; we embrace greater awareness, conscious choices, and deliberate actions with an open mind and heart.

The focus of a conscious lawyer is on being:

- *an enabler* – ensuring others fulfil their potential;
- *a facilitator* – creating the optimum environment for learning and growth; and
- *a coach* – holding space for the people around us to grow, learn, and contribute at their highest level of contribution.

When we operate as high-performing lawyers, we achieve exceptional results, recognition, and reward. But our capacity is limited to the extent of our inputs until achieving the same results each year becomes increasingly harder to manage. Many of us opt to simply soldier on, dig in deeper and compromise on personal goals in favour of professional survival. But as disruption and global uncertainty continue to challenge the legal sector in terms of the need for new business models, innovative solutions to meet client demands, and better talent retention capabilities, leadership transformation is becoming a necessity. There is no better time than now to take the courageous leap to becoming a conscious lawyer.

Chapter 2

Leading through change

Across every industry, technology is becoming increasingly disruptive, global competition is intensifying, generational shifts in the workplace are complicating organizational culture, and changing attitudes about corporate governance and responsibilities are putting pressure on leaders to change. The legal sector is changing in radical ways. Compounded by the challenges posed by the Covid-19 pandemic, law firms and in-house legal teams have faced market uncertainty, rapid calls for technological innovation, and upheaval in traditional ways of working with colleagues and clients.

The changing role of the in-house lawyer

The role of the in-house lawyer has fundamentally changed. Gone are the days of viewing the in-house team as lawyers who execute and reactively troubleshoot. Legal departments have shifted their brand from business adviser to strategic business enabler impacting all corners of businesses. Whilst legal teams have traditionally advised on ethics, governance, and compliance, the significance of their role has increased as boards place greater emphasis on good governance. Functions such as IT and marketing, historically viewed as operational, have been elevated to strategic level as businesses look to monetize their data and capitalize on their brands. The in-house team plays a major role in influencing and leading these strategic initiatives. The rise of the project management office to create greater efficiencies and transparencies in performance reporting has also intensified the role of legal in demonstrating value. In-house lawyers have also become risk takers as much as risk mitigators as they find innovative ways to deliver legal services to enable better, more responsible business.

This means that in-house lawyers have become strategic decision-makers who commercially influence and decide rather than being limited to advising on legal issues. Whilst in-house teams retain their traditional role as moral compass for the businesses they serve, they must balance ethics with business enablement, looking to unlock capital and contribute to revenue generation as much as protect reputation and brand. As business cost centres, they also have to demonstrate continued budget savings and efficiency and productivity gains through process enhancement and leaner resourcing. Put simply, they have to do more with less.

The Covid-19 pandemic led to the acceleration of digital transformation strategies to maintain business operations, and legal departments have been at the heart of organizational systems change. A primary focus of most recent change for the in-house team has been the need to demonstrate innovation in workflow, operations, and delivery through contract life cycle management, automation tools, and other process reinvention.

The *2021 State of Corporate Law Departments* report (Thomson Reuters Institute, 2021) found that, to ensure delivery of strategic goals, 81% of in-house team hirings in 2020 were for legal operations roles, an increase from 57% in the previous year. The same report found that the highest priorities of the in-house team were:

- controlling outside counsel costs (89%);
- driving efficiency in delivery of legal services (74%);
- focusing on internal data security (74%);
- using technology to simplify workflow and manual processes (61%); and
- focusing on legal operations (52%).

Recent trends suggest that in-house teams are channelling less of their legal spend towards law firms. Instead, they are adjusting staffing requirements in favour of temporary staffing solutions (secondments, consultancy arrangements, temporary contracts) and directing legal department operations professionals to conduct financial planning, project management, and outside counsel management. They are choosing to insource work and adopting new technologies to streamline legal services delivery through automation of operational workflows and contracts, and better document management systems (Greentarget, 2017).

The biggest threat to law firms, therefore, appears to be the corporate in-house legal teams they serve. Law firms have no choice but to innovate in how they deliver legal services to these clients.

What law firms are facing

Law firms are facing challenge from all directions (refer to Table 2.1 for a summary).

Table 2.1 What law firms are facing and the consequences

Conditions	Threat to the firm	Impact on the firm	Opportunity for the firm
Economic turbulence, regulatory uncertainty, and geopolitical instability	Big Four multidisciplinary services	Limited ability to respond and provide fit-for-purpose solutions	Forge collaborative partnerships and consultancy arrangements to provide bespoke client solutions
Erosion of client loyalty	Lateral moves and market consolidation of boutique teams	Growth of lawyer personal brands	Develop more strategically focused business development and client relationship strategies
Increasing pricing pressure	Buyers' market	Need to provide high-value services at the lowest cost possible	Develop intelligent, data-driven pricing using dedicated pricing teams and tools

Streamlined, efficient legal operations	Alternative legal services providers and a rise in insourced services	Reduced spending on law firm services	Offer the services of data analysts, legal technologists, and specialists in project management and legal operations
Greater reliance on technology, artificial intelligence, cybersecurity, and data privacy	Big Four multidisciplinary services and a rise in insourced services	Reduced spending on law firm services	Provide services through partnerships with technology vendors
Changing employee motivations	Shrinking talent pool	Failure to retain top talent	Achieve greater employee retention through policies that enhance mental health and wellbeing

The *2020 Law Firm Business Leaders Report* (Thomson Reuters Institute, 2020) states that in response to these challenges, 94% of respondents would probably, or definitely, increase their use of technology to improve law firm performance over the next year. Nearly 75% of respondents said they planned to make greater use of technology to cut costs.

Some law firms are responding quicker than others to gain competitive advantage by looking for greater technology efficiencies in legal services delivery. These firms are pursuing innovative approaches to meet client needs – for instance, seeking partnerships with technology providers in the arena of artificial intelligence and expert systems to build custom applications that can provide services to clients without lawyer time. According to a recent report (Lexis Nexis, 2021), while the billable hour remains an important part of the law firm business model, a material and increasing proportion of revenues accrue from other sources. The same report found that over 50% of revenues came from new non-billable hour sources, such as fixed-fee contracts, subscription-based services, and productization, suggesting a trend towards technology uptake (Lexis Nexis, 2021, p. 6).

This level of disruption, however, has revealed a significant skills gap among leaders of law firms. Lawyers who were traditionally measured according to their technical legal skills and ability to develop client relationships are now expected to innovate client solutions and create new business models. Many of these lawyers lack any background in digital transformation projects and integrating services with technology solutions. They may have learnt how to read financial spreadsheets, but many lack the requisite business expertise of their commercial counterparts in client organizations. In some senior quarters of the legal profession, a sizeable degree of upskilling and reskilling would have to be done to effect radical change in legal services delivery. This skills gap becomes even more problematic in the context of how these traditional lawyers can meaningfully influence and motivate the new generation of lawyers through these changes.

The new generation of lawyers

It is widely held that the new generation of lawyers in the workplace have different expectations and motivations to those who lead them. Most partners and senior in-house lawyers today are Generation X, born in the late 1960s and 1970s and growing up in economic boom times that encouraged independence, self-determinism, and mobility. The new generation of lawyers are Millennials, born in the mid-1980s and 1990s and living their twenties and thirties in a time of rapid global change and technology dependence. Now, in the early 2020s, Generation Z are principally teens or in their early twenties and just starting to enter a workplace struggling to keep up with global challenges.

The new generation have a reputation for being high maintenance in the workplace. They have been referred to as 'children of praise' as, in many cases, parents boosted their self-esteem by rewarding them for how smart and talented they are rather than for demonstrating initiative, effort, resilience, and passion for learning (Dwek, 2017, p. 136). They are viewed by some as having high opinions of themselves and high expectations of their employers. Espinoza, Ukleja, and Rusch (2010) offer suggestions for how to get the most out of this generation at work. According to them, Millennials demand access to decision-making, immediate feedback, praise and recognition, creative and interesting challenges, and complete autonomy. Generation Z may be even harder to motivate. Whilst Millennials grew up with limited internet access, Generation Z grew up in a 24/7 technological world. They might struggle to focus simply because they have grown up subject to multiple distractions and crave constant gratification and instant updates.

It appears that traditional management techniques cannot respond to the motivations and expectations of the new generation. Traditional command-and-control leadership ('it's my way or the highway') can send Millennials running out the door. Those who grew up with continual praise may have high opinions of their own capabilities and may not respond well to criticism. Generation Z, on the other hand, are often viewed as multitasking fast learners who are capable of learning autonomously or through efficient nontraditional routes. They are seen as more entrepreneurial and able to thrive in independent work environments (Wittebrood, 2021).

The new generation are attached to their digital devices. Having always had access to the internet offering continuous, unlimited information at their fingertips, they tend to look for answers to any and every question. As a result, they are often motivated to understand the 'why' before they are willing to commit to the 'what'. They can be more focused than many of the older generation on social justice and meaningful impact. Motivated to be part of something much bigger, they demand deals, transactions, and projects that deliver purpose (Espinoza, Ukleja, and Rusch, 2010). These Millennials focus on having a job that allows them to make an impact on the lives of others as well as live a desired quality of life. They work best as a team, and they love nothing more than a 'work family' culture. Generation Z, on the other hand, are viewed as more entrepreneurial at a younger age. Instead of committing to large corporates or law firms, many want to create start-up businesses that will allow them to work independently towards their life goals. It is not surprising, therefore, that traditional leadership structures and business models are cracking under pressure (Wittebrood, 2021).

Put this in the context of growing life expectancy. As of 2020, 50% of children born in the West have a life expectancy of 105 years (Gratton and Scott, 2020, p. 2). To create the necessary options for this longevity, Gratton and Scott (2020) argue that we need to replace the traditional three-stage life – education, work, retirement – with a multistage life. This will mean working beyond the traditional retirement age, but with a better balance of revenue-generating work, healthy activities, fulfilling relationships, and happiness. This multi-stage life is created through people having several careers with various transitions and breaks to recharge and learn new skills, bringing greater meaning and purpose in their lives.

This multistage lifestyle certainly seems to match the moti-vations and expectations of many of the new generation of lawyers. It comprises an explorer mindset that values youthful pursuits which enable people to experiment, play, change, and grow. It allows them to amass experiences that align with their values, interests, and skills sets. It also envisages new forms of entrepreneurship where workers are encouraged to work independently to exploit specific opportunities rather than sit below the umbrella of full-time employment and salary. As well, it envisages a portfolio lifestyle where people are incentivized to fulfil their passions and purpose through a combination of activities, such as working, volunteering, and pursuing personal hobbies and interests.

It seems that with the disruptive trends in the legal sector, departure from the traditional billable hour model and a move towards greater flexibility in resourcing and increased digitization of legal operations are being demanded not only by external global pressures but by lawyers themselves.

Barriers to change

Whilst change is being demanded by external and internal forces affecting our businesses, one of the biggest barriers to this change appears to be senior lawyers themselves.

Under the traditional law firm business model, leadership is not critical to law firm success. With an emphasis on quality of input, traditional lawyers would adequately manage the skills required to deliver strong financial results – technical expertise, ability to delegate and project manage, and monthly billing and lock-up. With increased disruption affecting the way law firms and legal departments operate, senior lawyers cannot simply manage; they must lead. The leadership skills required to successfully grow businesses are evolving radically. However, transformation of leadership behaviour is not keeping up with this rapid rate of change.

There is evidence to suggest that even though leaders in most law firms recognize that the landscape is changing, they are yet to adopt any dramatic changes in their behaviour in order to meet these new challenges. When law firm leaders were asked why they were not putting more effort into changing the way they deliver legal services, most reported that their clients were not asking them to or that there was not enough economic pressure to justify changes to the delivery model (Greentarget, 2017). Put simply, there was no sense of urgency to change. In addition, 64% of law firm leaders said the most significant barrier to change was resistance to change by partners themselves. Only 4% of law firm leaders saw their partners as highly adaptable to change (Green-target, 2017). Such low levels of adaptability and urgency for change indicate a need for cultural shift at top level to effect radical change in legal services delivery.

Leadership skills for leading through change

An article (Catalino and Marnane, 2019) on the hidden benefits of leadership programmes for women throws some interesting light on the leadership skills required to meet future global challenges. The article reports that of nine leadership behaviours which are highly applicable to future global challenges, two are exhibited equally by men and women, five are mainly exhibited by women, and only two are mainly exhibited by men. These are set out in Table 2.2.

Table 2.2 Leadership behaviours exhibited mainly by men and/or women

Exhibited mainly by men	Individualistic decision-making Control and corrective action
Exhibited equally by men and women	Intellectual stimulation Efficient communication
Exhibited mainly by women	Provision of inspiration Participative decision-making Expectation setting and provision of rewards People development Role modelling

Source: adapted from Catalino and Marnane (2019)

According to the latest figures on gender in the law profession in the United Kingdom, whilst women make up 52% of qualified solicitors, they make up only 35% of partners in law firms (Solicitors Regulation Authority, 2022). A recent survey of law firms in the United Kingdom found that women make up only 23% of equity partners (Tillay, 2021). With women occupying less than a quarter of decision-making roles in law firms, there is no wonder that law firm corridors of power still feel like bastions of command-and-control leadership.

Whilst the article by Catalino and Marnane (2019) suggests that it is mainly women who exhibit leadership traits necessary to lead through transformational change, it does not necessarily follow that this is only a gender parity issue. There is no doubt that change will come with greater promotion of women at board level. However, this article suggests that both men and women must utilize the right leadership toolkit to ensure that the businesses they lead are ready and able to advance radical change in the legal sector.

Look again at the skills required to lead through global challenges that are displayed more commonly by women. These relate to *how we impact the people around us*. With disruption, challenge, and generational shifts in the workplace set to continue, to be a leader of the future, all lawyers, regardless of gender, must take conscious steps to lead people through change.

Chapter 3
Choosing CARE

Leading people through change means changing the way we behave as leaders. We must shift our attention from delivering results to helping others achieve beyond expectations. This means greater focus on 'us' rather than 'me'. This also means changing the personal imprint we make on people when we are with them.

This chapter introduces you to my CARE model – a four-leap process that takes you through the shift from leading high performance results to unleashing untapped potential in people. When we are leading others through uncertainty and challenge, the more we care, the more open people are to change.

The need to be client-centric

My career has taken me from international 'magic circle' lawyer (BigLaw) to general counsel at a regulatory authority (in-house) to COO of a new model start-up virtual law firm (NewLaw). What I learnt most from this journey is how much my attention had to shift from being service-centric ('What services do I provide?') to customer-centric ('What do my clients need?').

During my time as general counsel, I was shocked at how little interest private practice lawyers showed in how my organization was run, the challenges we faced, and the strategic initiatives we prioritized as a business. Prior to launch of a new panel process, I made a point of meeting with the relationship partners of each incumbent panel firm to set the scene for why I was choosing to refresh our legal panel. In one such discussion, I observed with interest how SK, a newly appointed relationship partner, conducted the meeting. SK talked at length about the services her firm provided, the high-profile deals recently closed, and the internal changes in leadership and personnel in the region.

Over the course of 45 minutes, SK failed to ask me one single question. The conversation was entirely one-sided. I drew the meeting to an end early, without discussing the impending panel process. Her law firm was ultimately not appointed to the refreshed legal panel. The feedback I received from my team assessing applications was simply that SK and her law firm failed to demonstrate the curiosity required to work with us to deliver legal services differently.

The changing demands that general counsel have for alternative resourcing solutions, legal operations support, and integrated technology solutions require questions to be asked, options to be considered, and solutions to be created and developed to meet bespoke circumstances. Corporate legal departments need their law firm partners to step to their side to understand the practical needs of their organizations and the broader context of the legal services being delivered. A high-performing lawyer focused on delivering the highest quality of service is no longer sufficient. Instead, corporate legal departments are looking for service providers who operate collaboratively. They want their go-to law firms to be available between deals as much as on deal to proactively problem-solve, innovate, and curate credible options as challenges unfold. In fact, it is how law firms behave off-deal that cements a sustainable relationship.

My shift to NewLaw enhanced my perspective on what it is to adopt a customer-centric approach. NewLaw firms understand the need to radically reinvent the law firm business model to meet the varying needs of their clients. Traditional legal services delivery is replaced by digital transformation projects and alternative technology solutions. Lawyer hours are replaced by virtual retainers and alternative resourcing arrangements. The billable hour is banished to make way for fixed-fee contracts, subscription-based models, and productization (Lexis Nexis, 2021, p. 6). The most successful NewLaw firms anticipate the needs and wants of their clients, strategic partners, and intermediaries. They are more strategic in their thinking, pursuing opportunities in terms of 'us' instead of 'me'. They understand that growth lies not in winning at the cost of competitors but in partnering with others to achieve collaborative success. This means that when a client has a problem, the NewLaw firm looks at leveraging their relationships with other NewLaw partners – technology providers, accordion law firms, specialist sub-consultants – to offer a consolidated offering that fits the required solution.

Whether in BigLaw or NewLaw, law firms need their lawyers to be curious, adaptable, and resourceful. This is a different style of leadership, a people-centric, creative approach to delivering legal services differently.

The need to be human

When I reflect on my evolution from doing high performance at Level 3 leadership (production) to Level 4 leadership (people development) as a general counsel (Maxwell, 2013) and later, as a COO of a NewLaw firm, consciously choosing a different way to lead, I think clearly in terms of the leaps I had to make. It was a process of rehumanization.

As highlighted in Chapter 2, the new generation of lawyers need leaders to step up to a higher level of integrity that seeks greater meaning and higher purpose. This ascension requires a shift from treating business as a vehicle to compete and win, to seeing it as a commitment to serve people and uplift communities. It requires leadership that puts values and purpose front and centre of business strategy and replaces pursuit of profits and results with focus on process and impact for future gain. It means putting people first, redefining our criteria for success from financial gain to improving experience, and viewing performance as learning.

The Future of Jobs Report 2020 (World Economic Forum, 2020) refers to a new equilibrium in the division of labour between human workers, robots, and algorithms. It reports that whilst robots and artificial intelligence will become the mainstay of work across every industry, the creation of 'jobs of tomorrow' will still outpace the number of jobs lost. The ever-decreasing pool of legal secretaries, for example, will soon be replaced by the emerging fleet of data analysts and design engineers. But what is interesting here is not that our job roles will change; it is that we will add greater value. Looking at the professional services sector specifically, the report states that the top five emerging skills in this sector will be analytical thinking and innovation, complex problem-solving, critical thinking and analysis, creativity and initiative, and active learning and learning strategies. What this means is that as the role of the machine rises, what makes us unique as human beings – our ability to think strategically, relate, apply human judgement – will become our strongest differentiator. Whilst machines are great at doing, people are best at being. The future will require us to be more human in the workplace. That means the future of law will require its lawyers to be more human.

How the CARE model can help

The core difference between machine learning and human learning is that, unlike machines, people *care*. It is our connection to something bigger – a collective responsibility – that cements our will to do better, to improve, to gain. It is also our concern for not negatively impacting others – specifically, not causing them harm – that motivates us forward.

But to move forward in leadership is not a straight path. Indeed, when I look back on my journey from doing high performance to being a conscious leader, it has certainly not been a linear process. It did, however, have four distinct aspects.

The first aspect involved connecting to the leader inside me. At the beginning, I needed to simply get back to who I really am and discover the girl I once was. The impenetrable armour from private practice had to be stripped down, layer by layer, to uncover the simplicity of vulnerability and fear that we, as humans, all have.

What helped me make this shift was the second aspect – connecting to the 'why' by awakening my purpose. I had to deeply explore what I wanted in my life and work. I had to look beyond the trappings of a successful career and relationship and answer the simplest of questions: what is the point of it all? When I opened myself up to the suggestion that there is, in fact, a higher purpose to our individual contributions, progress started to flow.

I then had space for the third aspect – relating to others at a human level. It became less about 'me' and more about 'us'. When I started to explore my connection to others – relationships, influence, service – I started to recognize the actual impact I could have on others if I drew my attention to that. And I started to focus less on awareness of me and more on the experience of others.

Only then was I ready to open up to the fourth aspect of change – entrusting others to fulfil their potential. I had to let go of control entirely. I had to finally trust other people to learn and grow, and surrender myself to that process.

In the chapters that follow, I describe, as best I can, the process of evolution from doing high performance to being a conscious lawyer. The model I have developed and use in my coaching practice to help lawyers pioneer change in legal services delivery describes a process of four leaps, shown in Table 3.1.

Table 3.1 The four essential leaps from doing high performance to being a conscious lawyer

Leap I	*Connect* to the leader in you
Leap II	*Awaken* your purpose
Leap III	*Relate* to the people around you
Leap IV	*Entrust* others to fulfil their potential

Leap I: *Connect* to the leader in you

In the discussion of Leap I in Chapters 4 to 7, I explore the initial phase of evolution from high performer to conscious lawyer. For me, it started with the need to submerge my ego. After a prolonged period of operating at high performance level, I had started to confuse my success, recognition, and financial status with my actual identity. I had to learn that how I see myself is not how others see me and that what I have achieved to date is not my true value. I had to go on an inner journey to rediscover who I am as an individual and as a leader.

The process of discovering who we are is, itself, elevating. We often talk in terms of being a 'brand', but we falter when we focus on external perception of that brand rather than the experience people have of us in the flesh. Living our brand means working on our interactions with people every day and growing into ourselves through that process.

In the chapters on Leap I, I also set out the case for values-based leadership and the importance of aligning our behaviour with our inner convictions. When we know our core values and what they look like in action, we can make conscious choices in how we respond and act.

The chapters on Leap I would not have been complete without me covering those other aspects of our ego-selves that hold us back: our pursuit of perfection, our blind spots, and our need to find empathy and compassion. I describe the process of committing to uncovering the hidden parts of ourselves and taking time to better understand and appreciate them for how they serve us. And when we do that, we finally have the courage to take down the mask and be exactly the leader we are.

Leap II: *Awaken* your purpose

Leap II is the next call to action. This is discussed in Chapters 8 to 11. When I look back on my personal transformative journey, I would not have had the courage to switch from controlling results to giving conscious attention to people had I not connected to a higher purpose that I wanted to fulfil in my life and work. Whilst I had been leading through change for much of my career, it was not until I uncovered a passion for helping others to transform how legal services are delivered that I was able to connect to an urgency to change from profit to purpose.

The process of awakening purpose requires a fundamental shift in the mindset that our abilities are in any way fixed, limited, or scarce. In place of limiting assumptions about our potential, we must embrace the guiding truth that leadership requires a lifetime of learning. Acquiring the leadership behaviours needed to hasten the future of law is an ongoing process of change. It requires every leader to shift focus from pursuing outcome to facilitating progress.

Leap II is an evolving process through life. It requires an equilibrium state of challenge and ability – a flow experience. It is the constant attention to what is happening in the present moment of now. It is a practice of observing what is and not wishing it were different. Fulfilment comes not from reaching the destination; it comes from enjoying the beauty in the journey we are on. Leap II is probably the most self-enriching stage of all.

Leap III: *Relate* to the people around you

In the discussion of Leap III in Chapters 12 to 14, I deepen the discovery of what it means to shift focus from producing high performance results to empowering the people around us. It starts with acknowledging the financial and human cost of poor leadership. We have all experienced toxic workplace behaviour in our careers, but are we truly aware of the impact it still has on us once we ourselves sit in senior positions?

The process of drawing attention to impact on people requires us to step up to a higher level of integrity. When I talk of being more conscious, I mean we become more thoughtful and deliberate in our embrace of our roles and responsibilities. I draw on my own experience as well as the experience of many coaching clients to expand on what it is to make the fundamental shift from doing management to being a leader.

The chapters on Leap III provide an overview of the role of the conscious lawyer as enabler, facilitator, and coach. The conscious lawyer relinquishes control over outcome and instead focuses on creating the optimum environment for people to fulfil their highest potential. This involves transforming performance from task completion to flow activities and engaging people in progress and improvement. It becomes, of itself, a process of experimentation and learning to allow others to deliver at their highest level of contribution.

Leap IV: *Entrust* others to fulfil their potential

Leap IV, the final aspect of leadership transformation, is discussed in Chapters 15 to 17. This requires the bravest step of all: the leap of trust. Through my own journey of leading high-performance teams in legal, compliance, and governance, I have learnt that we cannot build trust in others until we first build trust in ourselves and believe in our own ability to change. This means we must make room for growth in ourselves as well as in those around us.

When we accept that performance and learning are one and the same, we start to see the experience of learning itself as the desired outcome. We make room for mistakes, course corrections, and new learning. Free from the shackles of ego, we transfer ownership of potential back into the hands of the people around us to empower them to step up to greater accountability and value.

If we are truly committed to being values-based, purpose-driven leaders of change, we must switch our role from commanding authority to granting autonomy. This means finding every opportunity to decentralize our decision-making and support the people around us in their journeys to being leaders of the future. When we empower the people around us to make choices, we grant them ability to succeed beyond limits.

If you want to courageously lead high-performance teams into the future of law, you must *Connect* to the leader inside you to *Awaken* your true purpose. Only then will you start to *Relate* to the people around you on a deeper conscious level and *Entrust* them to fulfil their highest potential. The chapters that follow will explain how to do just that.

LEAP I:

Connect to the
leader in you

When you dissolve your ego
And lead from a place of deeper self,
Others see the light that shines within.

And when you shine that light for yourself,
And you alone,
You radiate, you shimmer, you glow.

And others see that ray of light as
a beacon of hope
That lights a path of change in them.

That emboldens them to connect to
their own light
And take their first step into the unknown.

Change in you changes everything.

Chapter 4

Why egos crush souls

Connecting to the leader in us means connecting to who we are from the inside out: our essential sense of self. When we turn our attention inward to uncover who we are at our very core, we may be surprised at what we find. Who we are is not *who we tell ourselves we are*. Leap I begins with the need to go below the surface of our ego-selves. When we take that step, we soon discover how staying at ego level inevitably holds us back.

When ego serves us

Ego – our own sense of value or worth – serves us very well in our lives and our careers. It gives us drive, ambition, a strong sense of where we want to be. It lets us stretch beyond our reach, inspires us to follow our dreams, and allows us to aspire to achieve our future goals. It is ego that enables us to deliver at a very high performance level. When we operate from ego – a place of authority and command – we achieve strong delivery, successful results, and exceptional profits.

This egocentric approach to delivery has been viewed as the secret sauce for success in the legal sector. The idea is that when client relationships are built on reliability of work deliverables, there is no better way of ensuring consistent, high performance results than to cede power to the command and control of a senior lawyer. Clients love a personalized service and want to look to one person – one single point of ego – to deliver a final outcome.

Over time, however, if we allow our egos to go unchecked, if we permit them to overcome our reason and make choices for us, they can act against us and those around us.

How we see ourselves is not how others see us

It was around six months into my new role as general counsel. Hired to lead a whole-scale transformation of the legal function at a regulatory authority, I made sure I delivered some quick wins in my opening months – control over legal budget, strategic overhaul of outsourcing policy, and recruitment of top talent from the international market. My chief executive officer (CEO) took me aside for a mid-term performance review. He congratulated me and my team on our high-performance delivery; it was clear that we were elevating the status of the legal function within the organization to new heights. But the conversation that followed had an indelible impact on me personally. 'People don't like you', he said. 'I like you, because I know you, but I'm hearing that people find you intimidating.' I sat in silence, listening carefully to his words. I simply had no awareness of this. I asked: 'What is it that I'm doing wrong? I thought people respected me?' 'They are scared of you', he said. 'How will they come to you to ask for help or advice if they fear you?'

How we see ourselves is not always how others see us.

As high performers, we perceive ourselves as ambitious, determined, and strong-willed. We see these as positive attributes of strength and resilience. We often describe ourselves as systematic, attentive to detail, logical, and thorough. We pride ourselves on our sound judgement and consistency. The more extroverted among us are demanding and authoritative. The more introverted are diligent, thoughtful, persistent. As independent thinkers, we can be serious, directive, and extremely effective at delivering exceptional outcomes. As high performers, we can think quite highly of ourselves.

But others may perceive high performers differently. The independence and dominance of a high performer can be viewed as dogmatic, pushy, hard. Their tendency to take the lead can feel overbearing, intrusive, insensitive. Their drive and belief in their own judgement is often taken as intolerance for other views or, indeed, condescension. In cases where a team has been in prolonged high-performance mode with an egocentric boss, negative language pervades. Coaching clients describe to me situations where high performance leaders have been dictatorial, controlling, or aggressive. The term 'control freak' comes up repeatedly. They share examples of unreasonable demands or unrealistic expectations, and growing feelings of frustration and resentment. High performers can be perceived as arrogant, belligerent, or stubborn. In extreme cases, there is talk of loss of humanness and behaviour that is cold-hearted, thankless, robotic.

It is important as a leader to have a strong sense of self. However, where we falter is to confuse our achievements for who we are. When we view who we are through our ego-selves, we become detached from reality and proceed in pursuit of greater entitlement.

Shades of the dark triad

Tomas Chamorro-Premuzic (2019) poses a vital question that many of us have been asking ourselves for some time: Why do so many incompetent men become leaders? Based on his research, he lists three core reasons:

- our inability to distinguish between confidence (how good people think they are) and competence (how good people are);
- our love for charismatic individuals – leaders who are charming and entertaining rather than humble or boring; and
- our inability to resist the allure of narcissists who tap into our own narcissism.

In short, we create a surplus of leaders who are unaware of their limitations and unjustifiably pleased with themselves. They see leadership as an entitlement and lack empathy and self-control, so they end up acting without integrity and indulging in reckless risks.

Dutton (2013) goes one step further. He concludes that some professions attract people with psychopathic tendencies. Lawyers are second from the top on his list. CEOs are at the top. The list also includes surgeons, police officers, and clergypersons. It seems that any environment that has hierarchy and the opportunity to wield power and control over people will serve psychopaths well.

The draw to senior leadership positions would appear to apply to any one of the 'dark triad' personalities. Some characteristic behaviours of these personality types – narcissist, Machiavellian, or psychopath – are listed in Table 4.1 (based on Academy of Management Insights, no date). They have in common the core characteristics of lacking empathy and moral compass and using position to pursue selfish interests rather than organizational gains.

Table 4.1 Common dark triad behaviours as they translate to the legal sector

Behaviour	Narcissist	Machiavellian	Psychopath
Falsely takes credit for deal contribution	✓		
Actively self-promotes, internally and with external stakeholders	✓	✓	
Responds to negative feedback with blame, aggression, and criticism	✓		
Favours colleagues who massage and boost their ego	✓		
Selects battles based on service of their own needs		✓	
Controls or disrupts other people's influence	✓	✓	✓
Keeps information to themselves		✓	
Uses manipulation to reach goals		✓	✓
Schemes for personal gain irrespective of consequences	✓	✓	✓

Competes and does not collaborate or cooperate		✓	✓
Makes hasty decisions regardless of consequences			✓
Makes bold, risky decisions without regard to rules or ethics	✓		✓
Questions authority figures, rules, and status quo			✓
Bullies or blames team members to distract focus from the facts			✓
Tends towards inappropriate relationships at work		✓	✓

Source: adapted from Academy of Management Insights (no date)

Not all lawyers in senior leadership positions are fully paid-up members of the dark triad. However, we have all at some point in our careers worked for, or with, senior lawyers that show the traits listed in Table 4.1. These are the colleagues who operate from ego and are motivated by the power and opportunity that their positions offer. They can be arrogant, self-serving, and critical of those who do not see the world as they do. They are suspicious of change and manipulate situations for their own gain.

Often, the environment itself – high client demands, stressful deadlines, internal politics, and billable hour pressure – creates the conditions for these negative traits to thrive. We all have egos. We all want to prove our competence and worth, particularly in the face of competition.

Our latent characteristics loom large when we are under pressure to deliver results. The temptation to focus on selfish gain to feel more in control of our delivery can be too great to resist. When we feel weak or at risk, we can fall back on our titles and positions to exert pressure on others to deliver. When we are under extreme stress, feelings of unworthiness can overcome us and encourage us to blame or criticize others rather than face any suggestion of our own failures.

In the longer term, the cost of this impact is high. In Chapter 12, we explore the organizational and personal cost of toxic workplace behaviour. In a downward spiral of performance where fulfilment levels are low and attrition levels high, every year gets harder and the costs become greater until, finally, we reach the tipping point of unsustainability.

When ego stops serving us

Holiday (2017) explains how ego can wound us. In pressurized corporate environments, our egos can evolve from ambition to greed, self-esteem to arrogance, and confidence to superiority. In serving our ego-selves, we can become obsessed with being better than, more than, and recognized for. We measure our value by comparison to those we surround ourselves with, and we see others as means of serving our own self-interests.

You know when ego is controlling your leadership when the following behaviours show up.

As a leader, you are disconnected from 'what is'

Deeply self-absorbed and ensconced in self-importance, we can become completely detached from what is happening right in front of us. Listening only to what we want to hear and surrounding ourselves with people who silence themselves from dissent or critical feedback, we can become detached from perspective and truth. In this false sense of what is, we can acquire an overinflated view of our own significance and abilities, overestimate our value, and, in turn, devalue the effort and skills of the people around us who significantly contribute to our success. No longer interested in what is true, we become only interested in what we want to believe is true of ourselves. Because deep down, our biggest fear is failure.

As a leader, you act entitled

Mistaking our senior positions and titles or our stature as an identity, we can persuade ourselves that we are deserving of every advantage these may bring. We start to measure our success based on what others have and consider their success as coming at our own personal cost; this is sitting in scarcity mindset. We attract drama and conflict – making unreasonable demands, escalating conflicts rather than defusing them, and criticising and judging others to deflect from our own responsibility or mistakes. We do this because we are stuck in the lowest level of the hierarchy of needs (Maslow, 1943): the basic need of security. And because deep down, we fear that we are not enough and that one day we may be found out.

As a leader, you seek constant validation

Thinking that our senior positions are the sum of our self-worth, our primary concern becomes maintaining those positions at all costs. Focused on external factors to demonstrate our continued value, we become dissatisfied when we are not receiving constant praise and recognition for what we do. We start to search for opportunities that validate our worth – awards, accolades, followers. It is as if success does not happen unless someone sees it or 'likes' it. At its purest level, the validation is craved because, deep down, we feel we are not worthy.

When we lead ourselves from ego, we are leading ourselves from a place of fear. Fear that we are not enough, that we are not worthy, that we are fundamentally flawed, that we are unlovable (Hendricks, 2009) (self-limiting beliefs are discussed in greater detail in Chapter 8). Rather than deal with the discomfort of facing these beliefs about ourselves or parts of ourselves, we submerge or deny them or simply avoid treading near them. Instead, we cover up the pain and replace it with a much stronger force that can mask the hurt. We can pretend we are something else, better versions of ourselves that are perfect and worthy of all the riches and rewards we truly deserve. We create external versions of ourselves, masks that protect us from the world we face. And we use these masks both as shield and weapon against the outside world. With the masks upon us, we can face anything.

The authenticity gap

The concept of 'authentic leadership' is an emerging field in academic commentary and research (Gardner et al., 2011). There is a growing consensus about the core qualities of an authentic leader, which I like to sum up quite simply as 'knowing yourself'. The contrast between authentic-self and ego-self is described in Table 4.2.

Table 4.2 The contrast between authentic-self and ego-self

Authentic-self	Ego-self
Applies self-awareness	Is unaware of impact
Trusts thoughts, feelings, motives, values	Is dissociated from their self
Dedicates time to self-reflection	Sits in delusion on certain versions of truth
Seeks and responds to feedback	Denies, deflects, avoids feedback
Resolves conflicts openly and honestly	Orchestrates people and situations for personal gain

We often see the authenticity gap as a gap between who we are and how others see us. In truth, the authenticity gap lies between who we are and who we tell ourselves we are.

We listen to the inner critic – the negative messages about ourselves inside our minds – rather than sit in the uncomfortable feelings of what is happening in the moment of now (this is discussed in greater detail in Chapter 11). We select only the parts of ourselves we like and put our energies into building those aspects rather than dealing with the uglier, harder parts of who we are. By building up our egos to the exclusion of the hidden parts, we toughen up, we grow brittle, and we become inflexible. We do this to protect ourselves and our brands. And we become impenetrable, bullet-proof, the embodiment of our ego-selves.

Let's return to the story of my six-month performance review with my CEO. I was very lucky. This CEO is a conscious leader, someone who operates from empathy and compassion (we discuss choosing conscious leadership in Chapter 13). He cared enough to tell me where to start on the journey back to my authentic-self. 'Submerge your ego,' he said. 'Get out of your office and talk to people. Show them your human side.' When I returned to my desk, it was as if someone had turned on the lights. I started to observe the impact of my high-performance ways on my team and my colleagues. The nickname I had acquired by this point was 'the general'. I had worn this name with pride. I now realized that it was not who I really was; it was who I had become. I was dedicating my attention and energy to aspects outside myself to demonstrate my dominance, power, and presence. I would make demands of colleagues, take control of projects, and dominate committee meetings, telling myself that this was the best way to serve the organization. In fact, what I was really doing was disempowering, demotivating, and dehumanizing those around me. And what I needed to do now, above all, was turn my attention onto me – my thoughts, my feelings, and my behaviour.

When we lead from ego, we feel powerful. We feel strong and proudly show our worth in the form of bravado and resilience. This becomes a badge of honour for how we demonstrate our abilities as leaders. Our egos protect us from feeling vulnerable or being attacked. But when we lead from ego, our hearts are closed. We close off our vulnerabilities and sensitivities to protect ourselves from harm. The walls go up and we feel safe. But what stops us from harm also stops us from caring for ourselves and others. The walls are up so high that no compassion or vulnerability can cross them. We fail to show people love, and they cannot show their love in return. That is why we feel less human. That is why we behave like machines.

When we submerge our egos, our souls can breathe again. The walls around our hearts come down, allowing space for courage, empathy, and compassion. Rather than look outside ourselves for markers of value and success, we turn towards ourselves to measure the actual impact of our inter-actions and behaviour. And we start to see that who we are as leaders – our leadership brands – comes not from who we tell ourselves we are but from how we behave with other people every day.

Chapter 5

Being your leadership brand

When we shift from feeding our egos (who we tell ourselves we are) to nourishing our leadership brands (the unique elements of ourselves as leaders), we become who we are. For our brands to grow, we must be willing and able to change. Our brands are not what we achieve; they are how we make others feel when we interact with them. When we attend to the constant gardening of nurturing the relationships around us, who we are as leaders effortlessly evolves.

Your leadership brand

AD is a successful entrepreneur. As founder and CEO of her own law firm, she is a preeminent brand in her sector and has carved a reputation for championing diversity and inclusion. She portrays a strong image of being on top of her game and fulfilling all her professional ambitions and goals. Her LinkedIn profile supports this portrayal. It reads as a roll call of the promotional events she sponsors, the industry conferences she attends, and the awards she wins. As a legal brand, she shines bright. What she seems oblivious to, however, is how she is perceived by others who interact with her every day.

Leadership brands are not created through forced attempts to be someone we are not. We can complete the coveted MBA, acquire leadership credentials, and accede to the highest echelons of organizations without having the leadership qualities required to lead high-performance teams. This is partly due to the predilection we have for promoting incompetent male leaders (as highlighted in Chapter 4). But it is also largely due to our mistaken belief that we can and should fake it until we make it.

Change does not take place by coercing ourselves into being someone else. The paradoxical theory of change (Beisser, no date) states that change occurs when we become what we are, not when we try to become what we are not. It takes place when we take the time and effort to be who we are, to be fully invested in our current being and notice all parts of ourselves – even those that are contrary to what we like – and learn from that.

By forcing ourselves to see the parts of us that make us who we are, we create an overall picture based on what we know and what we may not yet know. Take, for example, the image in Figure 5.1. This suggests an overall picture of a complete circle even though parts of the circumference are unseen. This is the essence of the Gestalt approach, which holds that the whole is far greater than the sum of its parts (Perls, 1970).

Figure 5.1 The Gestalt approach: an overall picture even though parts are unseen

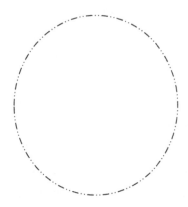

We cannot become who we want to be until we first become who we are.

By stepping into the role of who we are, we start working on closing the gaps from within. Change does not happen outside us, through building external versions of how we want to be perceived – a LinkedIn brand, a series of awards and accolades, a title, a position, a car, a house. Change starts from within. Whilst we must take actions outside ourselves that demonstrate what we stand for and what difference we want to see in the world, we cannot start with that alone. We need to start by evolving our own selves to create a stronger sense of who we are inside. And as the paradoxical theory of change says, when we work steadfastly from the inside out, we make meaningful and orderly change possible (Beisser, no date).

The problem with being a brand

When AD, the successful entrepreneur discussed above, reached out to me for coaching services, I was, at first, hesitant to work with her. Experience has taught me that for change to occur, clients must first be ready to change. Based on my interactions with AD, I felt it was not the right time. When I met her for an introductory chat, I asked, 'What is success for you now?' She shrugged her shoulders and said: 'I don't really know. All I know is that it's not enough. The more I achieve, the more I want.' The problem for AD was not that 'it's not enough'. The problem was that she was not enough for herself.

Through spending time with AD, I learnt a lot about the problem of being a brand. AD operated the controls of her role as if she were fully in charge. It was the inner critic in her head, however, who was controlling the operator (we discuss the inner critic in greater detail in Chapter 11). She would listen to the voices inside that told her she does not belong where she is, that her team members are ultimately after her job, and that it is only a matter of time before she is found out. She listened to the fear and altered her actions accordingly. She sought personal recognition for the successes of the firm, took every opportunity to publicly promote herself and her accomplishments, and generally did not trust her team to deliver without her direct involvement. Yet her self-esteem was such that she simply did not believe in herself. As a result, her team did not believe in her; they did not trust her leadership brand.

There are three core components of a leadership brand. Think about this in terms of a three-tiered pyramid, as shown in Figure 5.2.

Figure 5.2 The three tiers of a leadership brand

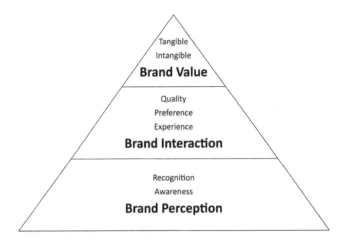

Bottom tier: Brand perception

The foundational level of a leadership brand is 'brand perception', or how we perceive a person from the outside. This comprises two parts:

- *Brand recognition* – recognizable features that identify a person as belonging to a certain brand. These usually encompass title, position, and role. The visibility of the brand has a large impact on our opinions of it. When the brand is commonly known – equity partner, general counsel – the perceived brand value is higher.

- *Brand awareness* – being aware of what a brand stands for. This can provide a level of familiarity that affects perception of the brand. For example, knowing that a person is chief legal officer of a financial regulator brings an understanding that this individual will be a financial regulatory expert and uphold the highest standard of ethics and integrity.

Whilst brand recognition is about what is on the outside, brand awareness is about what we assume is on the inside.

Middle tier: Brand interaction

The middle tier of a leadership brand is 'brand interaction', or how we experience a brand. This reaction will be subjective and is based on various factors:

- *Quality* – level of performance and what the person stands for. This is indicated by quality decisions, approach to ethics and governance, leadership qualities, type of culture they create, etc.
- *Preference* – alignment in behavioural style, beliefs, and values. For example, if a person suffered at the hands of a harsh female boss in the past, they may have a subconscious bias that leads them to favour male bosses.
- *Experience* – quite simply how that person makes us feel. If they listen, ask questions, and show patience and compassion, the impact will be positive. If they shout, have angry outbursts, or shame us in public, the negative impact can be long-lasting.

Top tier: Brand value

The top tier of a leadership brand is 'brand value', or the results of a positive or negative event. These can be tangible or intangible:

- *Tangible* – a result that is physical in nature and can be measured. An example is granting a team member a much sought-after opportunity.
- *Intangible* – a result that is nonphysical in nature and therefore cannot be assessed or tracked easily. An example is gossip relating to an inappropriate relationship with a colleague.

What this means is our leadership brands are only as good as our ability to support and maintain the top tier, brand value. Nourishing and maintaining positive brand value is principally about making our relationships thrive. We often put our energies largely towards the bottom tier – brand perception – as the elements are primarily within our control. But we derive the most return through nourishing the middle tier – brand interaction – by focusing on what others are experiencing as our leadership brands. Moments of negative behaviour, such as acting out in anger, betraying confidence, or excluding a team member from decision-making, can have damaging and lasting impact on our leadership brands. It can destroy trust, erode respect, and create resentment.

Shifting our focus from perception of our brands to actual experience of our brands starts with awareness of what the brand is: our brand promise. Brand promise comprises all aspects of who we are and what we stand for, including our strengths, our competencies, and our values (discussed in greater detail in Chapter 6). We have to commit to living up to the brand promise in our actions every day. For exercises in creating your own brand promise, visit www.kiranscarr.com/downloads.

When we are mindful of the experience of our leadership brand, we realize that being a brand takes constant attention to building who we are from the inside out.

Nourishing your brand

Working on who we are from the inside out means tackling three core components of who we are: our capabilities, our mindset, and our behaviour, as shown in Figure 5.3.

Figure 5.3 The three core components of who we are

Our capabilities

Our capabilities are not our qualifications, certifications, or track records of success. These may demonstrate our ability to hold certain positions or titles, but they do not equate to having certain leadership strengths, skills, and competencies and, therefore, value as a leader. That value comes from our actual experience of learning, understanding, and knowing. Unless we are present in the experience of building our capabilities – motivated and fulfilled by the actual experience of learning – we are simply checking off another tick box in the journey of being someone we are not.

Our mindset

True leaders have growth mindset. They adopt growth mindset to ensure they continue to close any authenticity gaps between who they are and who they tell themselves they are. This takes more than simply being open-minded and flexible. It means being dedicated to growing ourselves and those around us. It takes wholehearted commitment to cultivating our abilities and knowing we can learn from the collective wisdom of others (we deal more with adopting growth mindset in Chapter 9).

Our behaviour

Leadership behaviour requires alignment in thought, feeling, and action. When we think or say one thing and our actions say something quite different, the people around us know it. Behavioural alignment must exist regardless of whether anyone is watching. It is a state of being; it comes from within. We know we are in a state of alignment when doing the right thing becomes effortless.

Figure 5.3's virtuous cycle of being who we are will only continue to revolve when we work with all three components. Consider the leaders with different combinations of components in Table 5.1.

Table 5.1 Combinations of the three core components of who we are

Leader	Capability	Mindset	Behaviour	Impact
1	✓	✓		Loss of trust
2		✓	✓	Authenticity disconnect
3	✓		✓	Loss of impact

Leader 1 demonstrates capability and mindset without behaviour, leading to loss of trust

Based on some unfavourable feedback from his female team members, Leader 1 stretches out his fixed mindset to seek subconscious bias training and other leadership development courses. He is clearly focusing on his leadership capabilities and growth mindset. Once the training is complete, his team notice no change in his behaviour. Whilst he talks about some of the concepts he has learnt on his courses, he fails to alter his actions or decision-making to take account of this. His leadership behaviour is not aligned. The result is that his team lose trust in him.

Leader 2 demonstrates mindset and behaviour without capability, leading to authenticity disconnect

Knowing that there has been a major change in law requiring retraining and upskilling of lawyers to deliver up-to-date advice, Leader 2 arranges externally sourced state-of-the-art training for her team members. This is based on interactive case study learning and computerized tests of understanding. The team react extremely energetically and positively. She is clearly applying growth mindset thinking and aligning her behaviour accordingly. However, she chooses not to participate in the training herself, using the excuse of busyness. In truth, she would prefer to do the learning privately in case she receives a low test score. She elects not to participate in the full experience of learning with her team out of fear of how it might impact her brand. The result is that her team see her as unauthentic.

Leader 3 demonstrates capability and behaviour without mindset, leading to loss of impact

Leader 3 is sole equity partner of a multi-award-winning international arbitration practice that attracts and retains top talent and exceeds financial targets year on year. The expertise, experience, and strength of the entire team is unrivalled, and heavy investment is made to ensure they stay ahead of their competition. Leader 3 shows strong leadership capabilities for her high-performing team, and her leadership behaviour is thoughtful and consistent. The team members propose a shift in the practice business model, from traditional salary plus bonus to revenue share mechanisms, to better reflect the individual contributions of the top performers in the practice. Leader 3 rejects the suggestion outright on the grounds that the current model is not broken and works well for her. In short, Leader 3 is in a fixed mindset. The result is that the team see her as unwilling and unable to change.

We cannot do justice to our leadership brands until we accept that for them to grow, we must be willing and able to evolve as leaders. We focus on building tangible proof of superiority

– awards, press coverage, accolades – at the expense of what really matters. Being a leadership brand means nourishing and nurturing interactions with those around us every day. By attending to our interactions with the people around us, we come closer to closing the gaps between who we are and the leadership brands that we portray to the world.

Chapter 6

Letting your values speak

W ho we are as a brand comes down to our basic core values – what we stand for. What we stand for forms the bedrock of building trust, gaining loyalty, and generating repeat business and sustainable partnerships. If we want to be picked out from a crowd, it will be our values that differentiate us and give us our unique selling point. When we lead from values, we know who we are, and those around us know us too.

The case for values-based leadership

The corporate values of the international law firm at which NA was a senior partner were respect, integrity, collaboration, and excellence. As regional office head, NA had actively participated in the three-day strategy workshop that led to the creation of these guiding principles. He was passionate about his role in the firm and knew that his future lay in embracing this latest board strategy. He understood, from the coaching he had received, that the 'tone at the top' had to change to enable a cultural shift within the law firm so that it could live and breathe this refreshed set of corporate values. At partner meetings, he started to espouse the merits of collaborating across the network and leveraging cross-selling opportunities. He conducted personalized sessions with employees, explaining the rationale for the firm's move to values-based leadership and how it would radically change firm culture and performance. But after the initial flurry of the launch, NA operated much as he had done before. He continued as a lone wolf partner, competing with colleagues for file opening status on new matters brought in through collaborative efforts. He took credit for origination of files and the work of other partners, and when recording his time, he would retrofit according to his view of what time he ought to have spent on the file. To the outside world, he was the poster boy for values-based leadership. On the inside, however, there was a severe values deficit.

In these times of ever-evolving stakeholder demands, organizations have acknowledged that to maintain and sustain growth and profitability, they must create a set of corporate values that unites employees under one cohesive banner. A coherent set of core values operates as a culture manifesto that drives performance, decision-making, and interactions. It dictates the corporate brand, which encompasses behavioral standards, leadership competencies, and performance expectations. It is the foundation underpinning the 'why' of the organization, the bridge between having a vision and fulfilling it.

The effect of having a clear set of corporate values is that it binds employees to shared principles, greater collaboration, improved communication, stronger relationships, and better performance through fulfilment. Knowing that our colleagues are bound to similar core beliefs creates a sense of collective responsibility to perform, improve, and enhance the experience of everyone in the workplace. This, in turn, creates greater engagement, innovation, and retention – all of which lead to growth and profitability.

The problem that arises at leadership level, however, is that agreeing and communicating values is not enough. Values must be lived fully and consistently to effect meaningful impact on people and profits. To achieve this, the corporate values must align with the core values of the individuals who are leading the organization forward. But often, as we saw in the case of NA, leaders themselves are not values based.

When a leader's behaviour is not aligned with the values of their organization, people suffer. The values gap robs employees of trust, safety, opportunity, fulfilment, and dignity. In that deficit grows confusion, discomfort, fear, and conflict. In the case of NA, it took a number of high-profile partner exits before the global board took action against the absence of values-based leadership. But, regrettably, damage to the law firm brand had already occurred.

We all have different values that guide us through life. We can make choices that align with our values, or we can choose to breach values in the interests of greater gain or saving. As custodians of corporate values, senior leaders are measured against a higher standard of integrity. They must align their behaviour with their organizations' values and their own sets of personal values.

Being a values-based leader means being the soul of the organization.

Knowing your values

Knowing corporate values is one thing; knowing our own personal values and the role they play in the workplace is quite another. It can help to think about values as making up our own personal moral compass that guides our decisions in life. Consider them a general expression of what is most important to us. A life lived according to our values is a life lived fully from the inside out.

What is important to know is that values show up in the choices we make and in how we behave. Take this situation, for example: A team member accuses you of breaching trust by disclosing to the human resources department information told to you in confidence. 'I did no such thing!' you say, indignantly. You are surprised at how passionately you have responded in denial of their accusation. It may be because you have been triggered – that is, one of your core values has been breached. The accusation of having breached confidentiality may have challenged your core value of honesty, trust, or integrity.

These challenges face us every day, and we often do not pause to consider what drives our decisions to act and what happens inside ourselves when we react impulsively rather than think, reflect, and respond.

Think about a time when you reacted impulsively to an accusative statement by a colleague. What breach of your core values occurred in that moment of confrontation? More interestingly, were they upholding one of their own core values when they confronted you in that way? If they were, it helps to know that and view the situation with greater compassion (we discuss finding compassion in Chapter 7). If they were not upholding a core value, what was their motivation? Ego (discussed in Chapter 4)? Or a complete failure to connect to any values? Table 6.1 lists some key differences between values-based and values-deficit behaviour by leaders in the workplace.

Table 6.1 The contrast between values-based and values-deficit leaders

Values-based leaders	Values-deficit leaders
Act according to self-awareness	Act according to ego
Give praise and recognition generously	Harbour a sense of entitlement
Know themselves	Second-guess themselves
Make choices from curiosity	Make choices from fear
Align themselves to others for learning	Align themselves to others for gain
Act consistently	Make decisions erratically

Values-based leaders are highly attuned to their values. They know what their values are, they know what they look like in action, and they know how to align their behaviour to ensure their values remain uncompromised. We cannot avoid situations that conflict with our values entirely. Indeed, as lawyers, we are often final arbiters and decision-makers because of our skills in resolving the very issue of conflicting values. General counsel, by definition, provide the corporate moral compass, advising and guiding their boards on issues of business ethics versus business interests. There are no right answers in these situations. There is simply choice in how best to align our own values with those of organizations and stakeholders. There are exceptional cases where the compromise is too large for the leader to bear, and they choose to resign their position. But in most cases, we learn to connect to the essence of who we are and find the power inside of us to choose paths that can prioritize and reconcile the interests that matter above all.

Aligning behaviour with values

Have you ever looked your boss in the face and wondered why the lips are saying one thing and the eyes are saying something quite different? That is what can happen when a leader fails to align behaviour with values. What is happening in that moment is confusion; the conflict between speech and body language is telling you that trust is absent. The trick here, however, is not to judge the situation or the person. We often react and fall into default positions of judgement or criticism, particularly when we feel victimized. We mistake actions (what they did) for personality (for instance, being untrustworthy). In truth, it may just be that they have a different set of values to us. And they are honouring one of their own core values in their behaviour in that moment. Our values are not more worthy or better than their values. They are simply different.

Let us take an example. TS, a client, instructs you to commence due diligence and draft preliminary documents before a deal has been agreed in principle with his target counterpart. You are aware, based on previous dealings with TS, that he is a voracious dealmaker but a poor deal executor, often incurring extensive legal fees on deals that abort at early stages. You are under pressure from the regional head to improve practice profitability, and this revenue would certainly help your quarterly results. One of your core values is integrity, and as a matter of principle, you never commence work on a deal unless you feel there is a credible deal to execute. You raise your concern regarding premature commencement of work with TS. He dismisses your point, saying: 'Don't worry, I'll manage the board's expectations on your fees. You'll get paid.' You may consider that TS is acting from a place of values deficit, or ego perhaps. Alternatively, TS may be under extreme pressure to deliver and so feels compelled to uphold one of his core values: security. There is no clear right or wrong in this scenario – there is just a choice to be made. A leader must align behaviour with values. TS may continue to pressure you to commence preliminary work to secure progress of the deal. You can choose to align your behaviour with your values by refusing to proceed or commit to limited work that enables a headline term sheet to be developed to facilitate dealmaking. Either way, who you are as a leader is how you choose to put your values into action.

Knowing what your values look like in action

If our actions as leaders do not align with the values we espouse, our team members feel authenticity disconnect. In managing our choices in the moment, it helps to know and understand how our core values show up in us. We all have default reactions in different situations that derive from our personalities or behavioural styles, our genetic or cultural backgrounds, and past or present environments in which we have grown. Self-limiting beliefs account for some reactions, and stress levels also play a significant part in the workplace. It helps to know what we do when we choose to invoke our values or when they are threatened or challenged. We must know what our values look like in action.

It can help to develop a description of how we behave when upholding particular values (say, integrity) at home or at work to remind ourselves of the behaviours that are at risk of showing up in us when we are under pressure or challenge. Table 6.2 provides an example.

Table 6.2 Behaviors that uphold the value of integrity

I always behave with *integrity,* and this means:
<ul><li>I am open and honest with everyone.</li><li>I admit when I have made a mistake or changed my mind.</li><li>I do not rush to judge or challenge.</li><li>I do not blame someone else for what is ultimately my responsibility.</li><li>I will not 'go along' with something that goes against any of my core values.</li></ul>

This is such a powerful tool for everyday leadership. So often in reactive mode, we do not live the best version of ourselves. When a team member uncovers a mistake for which we are responsible, we opt for silence instead of admission of culpability. When we miss team deadlines, we can look for things outside of us to detract from our own omissions. When we lose cases, we like to discredit the decision-makers.

Reminding ourselves of the choices we can make to uphold our values creates stronger awareness of who we are. Having clarity on how to avoid dishonouring our values is even more powerful. It can protect our brand value and stop us from diluting our brands with one poor decision.

Knowing our values and understanding how they show up in us helps us to make choices that are authentic to who we are as people and leaders. For an exercise in knowing your values, visit www.kiranscarr.com/downloads.

Controlling your choices

As leaders, our choices, decisions, and actions are how we put our personal and corporate values into action. The average leader will make 35,000 plus choices per day (Hoomans, 2015). That is 35,000 plus daily opportunities to implement the values that we have.

Each reaction to a situation is a risk. The risk lies in failing to implement our values. We can reduce this risk significantly by moving from a place of reaction to a place of response. Response is to pause, consider which values we uphold if we proceed, or breach if we do not, then proceed to take steps in alignment with the values most in need of being upheld. We seem to love drama in the workplace. We are drawn to it particularly in these technological times of instant gratification and constant stimulation. But what we need above all in leadership is consistency. Teams, clients, and stakeholders respect us if they can see and predict patterns in our behaviour. They trust and respect us when we administer our autonomy and accountability in alignment with a moral code that dovetails with the best interests of the organization and its people.

When people around us know what our values are without us having to tell them, we are values-based leaders.

Chapter 7
Taking down the mask

When we know who we are – from the inside out – and keep growing into being ourselves, our leadership behaviour evolves. With this evolution comes greater courage to truly step up to a higher level of responsibility. We can finally take down the mask and be who we are.

Finding connection to greater consciousness

SD, the CFO of a regional company, was leading a multi-million-dollar financing deal. His team lacked relevant experience and competence in this area, and he was failing them as a leader. Anticipating that the deal was at risk of falling over, SD started to take steps to insulate himself from the fallout, sending accusative emails to the general counsel, copied to the CEO, reporting that the legal team was not supporting his team by taking ownership of their contribution. As leader of that legal team, the general counsel's reactive response would be to go on the attack to protect her brand and the brand of her legal team, unable to see the approach as anything other than a direct attack on her personally. This would be her ego showing up and telling her to respond in judgement and counterattack. But she was a conscious lawyer. She had learnt over time how to submerge her ego in the face of aggressive challenge. By connecting to who she is and what she stands for, she was able to invoke empathy for the CFO. She asked herself in that moment, 'How is SD feeling right now?' By stepping to the side of the CFO, she was able to view the situation through his eyes. And she saw his perspective. SD was scared, concerned, acting in fear. The general counsel knew from having spent time with SD that one of his core values was family. The significance of the deal falling over would certainly threaten SD's position as CFO, and he feared for his livelihood and that of his family, who he was supporting.

By submerging her ego and connecting to her whole self, the general counsel was able to act from a place of courage and compassion. Having reflected on context, she visited SD's office to have a very different conversation. She sat down beside him and said: 'I saw your email and I too am concerned about this deal. What can I do to help you?' What followed was an open discussion about the deal, the obstacles, and how they, as leaders, could collaborate to ensure their teams worked more effectively together. The general counsel left her preconceptions at the door. She was present in the moment of what was spoken, without fear or judgement. She focused on who each of them was and what they could do to achieve success together.

Who we are as leaders comes from inside us. Rather than focus on external factors that sit outside us, our attention must shift towards ourselves to explore what is happening inside us.

According to yogic tradition, we have seven spiritual centres, or chakras, inside our bodies, and these allow energy to flow freely through us. Imagine each of these as a wheel or vortex. Spiritual teaching tells us it is important to keep these energy centres open to allow energy to flow freely through us and inform the mind and body how to act and respond. When these energy centres are open, they rotate, creating flow of energy in the form of ideas, emotions, and feelings. Blocked or closed chakras can cause distortions within our bodies, such as emotional, mental, or physical ailments.

Take, for example, a situation at work when you suffer conflict with a difficult colleague. In the face of their sudden outburst, you feel anxious, unsure of what might occur, and you silence yourself until the colleague leaves the room. It is important at that moment to observe what you feel in your body. You may feel tightness in your chest or notice that your breathing is shallow and you struggle to catch your breath. This is telling you that your heart chakra is closed and your throat chakra disturbed. Perhaps you are frightened and need to protect yourself from harm; you have closed your heart to protect yourself. Maybe you feel it in your throat because you have silenced yourself; you are not speaking your truth.

By knowing the power of each chakra, we can connect to the power that lies within us. Table 7.1 sets out what I have learnt in my own journey of transformation from doing high performance to being a conscious lawyer. Each chakra operates as a source of power and gives me the energy to maintain a desired state of being in any moment of now.

Table 7.1 The seven chakras and their role in transitioning from high-performing lawyer to conscious lawyer

Chakra	Lesson	State of being	Process of transition
Crown	Spirituality	Having a vision for the future	From delivering results to unleashing untapped potential
Third Eye	Awareness	Being in flow of experience	From being task orientated to experiencing now
Throat	Communication	Being able to speak your truth	From relying on personal judgement to seeking advice and input
Heart	Compassion	Having courage to care	From demonstrating power to showing heartfelt courage
Solar plexus	Power	Having humility in service	From having a strong sense of self to submerging ego
Sacral	Creativity	Being connected to intuition	From absorbing pressure to investing in self-care
Root	Trust	Being grounded in yourself	From labelling success to recognizing achievement

In the example above, when the general counsel sat with the CFO, she consciously harnessed the power inside her. As a conscious lawyer, she believed in herself and trusted her judgement in situations of challenge and conflict (root chakra). She submerged her ego, which allowed empathy to rise inside her (solar plexus chakra). The space she created inside allowed her to connect to compassion; she sent signals to her heart to open (heart chakra). With the courage that came from a kind and brave heart, she was able to speak her truth (throat chakra). By opening the energy centres inside herself – shining her light – she gave SD permission to do the same. SD connected to his heart and his defences came down. He became open to speak his honest and vulnerable truth too. And they met in the middle without drama or conflict; they created abundance.

Starting with submerging ego

Through my journey, I have discovered that when we operate from ego, we feel strong, powerful, even invincible. But that power lasts only for so long, as it is fed from an external supply of recognition, rewards, achievement. Over time, as we crave greater demonstration of our power, this finite source of supply dwindles. We must draw more on external sources, and that power is commonly fed at the expense of others – their efforts, their kindness, their goodwill. The more we need, the more we deplete those around us, and diminishing marginal utility sets in. The more energy we expend, the more finite our power becomes.

When we submerge our egos, something quite different occurs. As my CEO told me after six months of high-performance delivery: 'Submerge your ego. Let the person that you are shine through.'

When we operate from a place of deeper consciousness, our power is self-sourced and infinite. It is a light that shines inside us constantly and without depletion of resource. It is self-nourishing and unending for as long as we practise connection to our whole selves. Table 7.2 contrasts what it feels like to act from a place of ego and a place of deeper consciousness.

Table 7.2 What it feels like to operate from ego-self and conscious-self

Operating from ego-self	Operating from conscious-self
Act from fear	Act from courage
Feel enraged by criticism	Seek open and honest feedback
Feel intimidated by the success of others	Find inspiration in the success of others
Want to win at all costs	See mistakes as enabling learning
Care about own opinion	Care about the opinions of others
Feel superior and entitled	Show humility and gratitude
Believe in certainty	Embrace uncertainty

How do we learn to submerge our egos and let consciousness rise, you may ask?

It starts with being comfortable in stillness. Sitting alone, silencing our thoughts, and being ourselves and only that. It is amazing how little we do that in our lives. When we sit in a taxi, in a waiting room, at home, we instantly choose an action to perform – we pick up our phone or a newspaper, or we turn on the television. Any activity to fill the empty void of nothingness in which we feel boredom, discomfort, or anxiety. In my case, it was a ski accident that triggered the need to stop. On the morning I was discharged from hospital, I was transferred to the couch in my living room. Sat there, legs extended in front of me, I realized that after eight years in my home, I had never actually sat on that couch. Never time to sit down. Ever busy doing life and work.

Choosing mindfulness – the state of consciously being in the moment of now – allows us to connect instantly to our deeper consciousness. This means:

- experiencing the now without thought of what it is or what it needs;
- avoiding judgement or attachment;
- seeing what we feel and not wanting something different;
- bringing mind, feelings, and soul into one;
- creating space;
- slowing pace;
- discovering stillness; and
- finding contentment from within.

Often, when we sit in stillness, thoughts about ourselves immediately pop into our minds. The inner critic says: 'How have you got time to sit down?' 'Why didn't you speak up more in the meeting this morning?' Mean talk that makes us feel uncomfortable. So we reach for our phone or attend to unnecessary tasks that we tell ourselves are urgent, to distract us from the discomfort of seeing the parts of us we do not like. This is the ego-self that gets in the way of who we really are. We deal with letting thoughts get in our way in greater detail in Chapter 11. For now, it is important to know that we can learn how to submerge our egos through mindfulness practice.

This takes many forms:

- gentle exercise, like yoga and pilates, which allows us to lose ourselves in the practice of connecting to physical parts of our bodies;

- rhythmic exercises, like long-distance running or cycling, which train our attention away from our thoughts to the rhythm of movement;
- walking in nature or by the ocean, which allows us to observe the enormity of beauty that naturally surrounds us and teaches us how insignificant we are on this earth;
- repetitive actions, like drawing, preparing meals, tending to a vegetable garden, which put us in the state of flow; and
- meditation, which allows us to enter the vast space inside ourselves in which lies our wisdom, our knowledge, and our power.

For an exercise in finding mindfulness practices that work for you, visit www.kiranscarr.com/downloads.

When we lead from a place of ego, we look outside ourselves for the source of our power. Our minds detach from our essential selves. When we submerge our egos, we connect back to ourselves – our one true source. We realize that true power lies deep within us and that we are able to tap into the limitless wisdom and energy of who we are.

Letting go of perfection

When I look back at how I behaved as a high-performing lawyer, my biggest struggle seems to have derived from my need to be perfect. Perfection was a constant pursuit. Nothing I did was ever good enough for me. My head was always full of what I should be doing instead of what I wanted to do. In the face of a big win, accolade, or award, all I would feel was that I needed to do more next time. It was in my role as general counsel that I learnt the destructive impact of my perfectionist ways. Until then, I had not fully appreciated how inflexible, uncompassionate, and unforgiving I had become. At times, this was directed outward, on my team and my peers. But, more significantly, it was directed towards me. The need to constantly prove myself was overriding my personality and performance. I would only focus on what was missing; I was never grateful for what I did, in fact, have. Being perfect was not serving me anymore. I had to let go.

Letting go of the idea of perfection is difficult. It is a process that takes patience and practice. It starts with becoming aware of the impact that the pursuit of perfection is having on how we behave; then we adjust our behaviour to secure different outcomes until finally we can embrace imperfection wholeheartedly. In Table 7.3, I explore the different feelings and actions that come to the fore when pursuing perfection and embracing imperfection. Letting go of perfection is truly liberating in all senses.

Table 7.3 The contrast between pursuing perfection and embracing imperfection

Pursuit of perfection	Embracing imperfection
Making decisions from a place of insecurity	Making choices from a place of curiosity
Controlling the mind through stress	Allowing the mind to observe how I feel
Feeling impervious to harm	Being open to fragility and vulnerability

Having a constant need to add more	Knowing how much is enough
Fearing that well-being will come to an end	Feeling joy in the moment
Looking back as indication of your future	Being present in the now
Obsessing on quality of detail	Focusing on impression and impact
'I must be the best'	'I know my potential is limitless'

In my journey of letting go of perfection, I stumbled on the writings of Suzuki (2021) on the Japanese philosophy of 'wabi sabi', ancient teachings that underpin Japanese art, history, and life. At its very essence is a tacit acceptance that perfection does not exist and imperfection is the only reality. What changes our experience of reality is learning to appreciate the value in the imperfect. This means training our minds to see that there is beauty in everything, even the broken, the incomplete, the decayed. This beauty may lie in appreciating what we had before it was lost, seeing the uniqueness in the chipped porcelain cup, or knowing the learning you have gained from making a grave mistake. All these examples are about looking for the positive in something so easily accepted as negative. Negative reality norm theory (by Carol Painter; see Crossroad Advantage, no date) suggests that society's picture of reality is set at negative: we are hardwired to see positivity as naïve and negativity as being better informed. This means we must take deliberate steps to switch to positivity in our field of vision. Lawyers, particularly, are hardwired to see what is wrong with a picture rather than what is right with it. It is simply how we are trained to think.

The good news is that it is possible to retrain our brains to choose gratitude for the imperfect. For an exercise in letting go of perfection, visit www.kiranscarr.com/downloads.

When we can see the beauty in what we have, we are ready to open our hearts to what we do not yet feel.

Finding compassion

I have always considered myself to be a kind and thoughtful soul. As a young girl, I was adventurous, spirited, and fun. My sisters would say I could find joy in a paper bag. As I grew up and racked up achievements in terms of school life, university, and early career, I started to submerge that side of me in favour of ambition, recognition, and reputation as a top performer. By the time I had reached the lofty heights of general counsel, I was a tough nut to crack. Years of working in egocentric, results-driven, male-dominated environments meant I had hardened on the outside and the inside. In fact, my heart was tightly closed. Operating in the ruthless environment of limited opportunity and endless pursuit of perfection, I was in full-body protective mode. I had put up walls around my heart so I could absorb unending volumes of work, deflect concern or criticism, and endure whatever was thrown my way without showing any weakness. One partner told me he thought I was cold and unfeeling. I shrugged my shoulders and told him it was his problem not mine. But what I did not realize then was that the greatest impact of putting up walls around your heart is not that the walls stop you from caring for others, but that they also stop you from caring for yourself.

It was not until I had my ski accident that I truly discovered the importance of self-care. I had become so strong and rigid in my high-performance armour that my knee finally buckled below me. I was sent on a long and winding journey of recuperation and reformation to learn about my unhealthy pursuit of being perfect, my inflexibility to challenge, my view of pain as weakness, and the need to forgive and let go of the resentment I held for past betrayals. I learnt that when I lead with a heart that is closed, I lead with strength. When I choose to lead with a heart that is open, I lead with courage.

The English word 'courage' derives from the French word for heart, *le coeur* – the core, the essential part of something inside. When we connect fully to our open hearts, front and centre of who we are, we are intrinsically connected to our whole conscious-selves. We tap into our instinct and intuition. Our judgement is sound and clear, and we act with decisiveness, because it comes from a place of belief and trust in ourselves and others. We are grounded in ourselves and make choices and take actions that align with our core values and beliefs. Instead of crushing souls, we light people up, we connect them to the power that lies within them, and we empower them to move ahead with vision and determination.

Reconnecting to my heart led me to the biggest lesson of all: compassion for others starts with compassion for yourself.

There are some simple truths in this:

- We cannot help others if we are running on an empty tank.
- Service to others in need starts with service of our own needs; it is self-care, not selfish.

- We must prioritize above all what we need to function – exercise, nourishment, space, time.
- We must surround ourselves with people who help and support us in meeting our priorities, and remove those who do not.
- We must take each day as it comes; decide what compassion looks like in the moment, and choose it.

In the beginning, I had to consciously program myself to make choices that showed compassion for myself. I would have to make myself sit down on my couch and do nothing. Just sit there in silence, nurturing whatever my need was – rest, nourishment, stillness. When I woke up each morning, I would have to send deliberate messages to my heart to say 'It's okay, you can open now.' Slowly, over time, I observed the difference it made to my behaviour each day when, first thing in the day, I chose self-care over the constant urgencies and demands of my role. In time, I had the courage to choose my self-care routine above everything until it became my default priority; I learnt to embody it. What urged me forward in this journey was seeing that I was becoming a better leader of myself, my family, my team, and my business.

When we open our hearts to compassion for ourselves, we free ourselves. The energy wheel of our heart chakra rotates at lightning speed and touches the hearts of those around us, telling them to open too. We take courageous steps towards other people. We reach out to them to explore new ground. We are open to asking what we do not know, looking for answers, and searching for undiscovered truths. Rather than sitting in the limited possibilities of fear, we step courageously into the arena of unlimited opportunities and possibilities, and we embrace the uncertain. Finally, we have the courage to uncover the hidden parts of ourselves that we have failed to touch.

Dealing with blind spots

We all have blind spots. Even the most self-aware among us have sides of ourselves that we do not see. It is because we all have baggage – the leftovers from our internal family dynamics, our cultures, our environments, our traumas, our experiences in corporate life. A key element of being more conscious is acquiring enough self-knowledge to better recognize our strengths and weaknesses, and take responsibility for their impact, positive and otherwise, on those around us. The good news is that there are tools available to enhance our understanding of ourselves and how we are perceived by others.

The Johari window (Luft and Ingham, 1955) can improve our awareness of ourselves and others in a group. It identifies four types of self, relating to awareness of our personality traits, characteristics, and qualities, as summarized in Table 7.4.

Table 7.4 The Johari window: the four parts of self and what they mean

Type of self	Extent of awareness	Potential impact
Open self	Characteristics of ourselves that we are aware of and are known to others	The more comfortable we are with ourselves, the more open we tend to be with others about who we are.

Hidden self	Characteristics of ourselves that we know about but which may be too private to share with others	More conservative or introverted individuals may be less willing to reveal information relating to their personal circumstances than those who are more liberal or extroverted.
Blind self	Characteristics of ourselves that others can see but which we are blissfully unaware of	We may limit ourselves by not nurturing attributes that we do not observe in ourselves (for example, being smart) even though others do.
Unknown self	Hidden depths within ourselves that nobody knows about, including ourselves	Our potential can be limited where abilities are underestimated or untested due to lack of opportunity, encouragement, confidence, or training.

When we embark on the process of uncovering parts of ourselves, we aim to increase the 'open self' by reducing the other selves as far as possible. The process of reducing our blind spots involves:

- *self-disclosure* – the need to communicate, open up to vulnerability, and become more approachable (without oversharing!); and
- *feedback* – seeking in-moment, factually based, open feedback on how we make a person feel, what we are not seeing, and what we should know. It is necessary to seek feedback not just from our direct reports but also from other stakeholders to understand what others are saying about us and our behaviour.

As we uncover more of ourselves, we understand ourselves better, allowing others to understand us better too. For an exercise in increasing awareness of how you are perceived, visit www.kiranscarr.com/downloads.

We all have blind spots regarding who we are and how we are perceived by others. Using tools available to us, we can build a picture of the gaps between our perceived value and the value we bring. To know ourselves, we must lose ourselves in the discovery of what lies unseen.

Having courage to take down the mask

Let's return to AD, the successful entrepreneur and law firm CEO from Chapter 5. AD's inability to let go of her external brand image was the limiting assumption inside her head that continually spoke 'you are not good enough'. Through our coaching work, we uncovered that this self-limiting belief fuelled her constant urge to compete with every person around her. AD had to learn to believe in herself before she could practise letting go of being the best (we discuss self-limiting beliefs and the role they play in scarcity mindset in Chapter 8). The biggest shift of all in AD's journey was finding compassion for those who had harmed her in her past. By dealing with the betrayals of her past, she was able to forgive herself for her own contributions (we discuss limitations of our past in Chapter 8). This made room for forgiveness towards others for their betrayals of her. When she opened her heart to acceptance of what had occurred, love for herself and others poured in (we discuss freeing ourselves from self-limiting beliefs in Chapter 9).

Free of these burdens, AD finally had courage to take down her mask completely. AD's LinkedIn profile no longer reads as a roll call of her many external successes. AD simply shares what she sees, feels, and learns as she consciously leads her team and business.

Courage to change comes from the heart. Only when we let down our defences and open ourselves up to our vulnerabilities, blind spots, and limitations seeded in the past are we able to accept ourselves for who we are. When we lower our expectations from being perfect to being human, we are better able to look truthfully at ourselves to see the whole sum of our parts. The journey from showing strength to being courageous is learning how to look in the mirror and love every part of ourselves, wholeheartedly.

The source of power as a leader comes from inside us. When we submerge our egos and turn towards the deeper consciousness that sits inside us, the power source is unlimited and bountiful. Grounded in our values and strong sense of who we are, we start to uncover and turn towards the parts of ourselves we may dislike or find uncomfortable. Motivated by learning, we have the courage to grow our capabilities, mindset, and behaviour to evolve our value. Until, finally, we have the courage to take down the mask and look up to see that there is a bigger purpose ahead of us if we are only willing to stretch beyond our reach.

LEAP I in a nutshell

- It is important as leaders to have a strong sense of self. Where we falter is viewing ourselves through our egos. We create authenticity gaps between who we are and who we tell ourselves we are. The more we operate through our egos, the more detached we become from reality. We lose connection to who we are; we become less human.

- When we make the shift from feeding our egos (who we tell ourselves we are) to nourishing our leadership brands (the unique elements of ourselves), we start to connect to who we are as leaders.

- Leadership brands are not created through forced attempts at being someone we are not – a 'fake it till you make it' approach. We must work on closing gaps from within. This takes constant gardening; we must work on three core aspects of who we are: our capabilities, mindset, and behaviour.

- We often put our energies towards how we are perceived externally, as brands. In truth, our brand value grows through working on our interactions with people every day. For our brands to thrive, we must be willing and able to evolve into who we are.

- Our values tell us who we are. When we align our personal values with our behaviour and implement them in the choices we make, we become values based. As value-based leaders, we also align our behaviour with corporate values and take steps to put those values into action in the conscious choices we make.

- By submerging our egos, we connect to our inner consciousness. We are able to let go of perfection and appreciate the true value and beauty in imperfection. We go in search of stillness and, with open hearts, we learn that compassion for others starts with compassion for ourselves. We are able to turn to those hidden parts of ourselves that we suppress or deny. As we understand ourselves better, we are more open to allow others to understand us too.

- Finally, we are ready to take down the masks that hold us back and uncover a greater purpose waiting to be awakened inside of us.

LEAP II:

Awaken your purpose

'Look within', she said, and I did.

And instead of focusing on the enormity of
what lay ahead,
I looked down at my shoeless
feet and smiled.

I took one step forward and then the next.

Within a few steps, I could move with ease.

With a lightness I had not felt before.

I felt courage within and a power so strong
I could accept all that is.

No thoughts of what might be.

Just a need to feel the way I felt then.

In that moment.

And allow it to engulf me, completely.

Chapter 8
Why results limit us

Through the journey of Leap I, we connect to who we are. Leap II centres around the question of why. We are so often focused on short-term performance results that we miss the fundamental purpose of our efforts. Only when we confront the need to relinquish control of results do we address a deeper calling to fulfil the unlimited potential that lies within us.

Competition is a scarcity mindset

In my experience, the most common outcome of corporate retreats was the lingering feeling that there were many people in the organization I did not know and, having spent some time with them, was less inclined to know. There would always be a swell of people who made it their sole intention to create impact in the eyes of the senior leadership team. Their objective was to shine, and the coming together of everyone would encourage their worst behaviours, like showboating brilliance, highlighting brutish strength, winning at all costs. And the immediate effect? Demotivating the majority. In the face of such unbridled competition, some would hide, some would shrink, and some would literally disappear (to an unavoidable work emergency). And the total impact? The performance level of the overall group was reduced. The race to the top had resulted in limiting the performance of everyone in the room.

Competition is healthy when it sharpens performance, encourages creativity, and drives people to do their best. If what we seek is for each person to actualize their potential, it makes sense to create an environment that pressures people to push themselves to their limit. But competition improves a person's performance only when their attention is focused primarily on the activity itself. If, however, the person is otherwise focused – on beating their closest rival or impressing their senior colleagues, for example – competition soon becomes a distraction rather than an incentive to focus attention on improving performance.

There is an underlying assumption that success is reserved for only the best. It is scarce and available only to the strongest and hungriest. But that is a lie. Whilst a seven-figure salary is reserved for a few at the top, what we earn is the narrowest of success criteria. Competition makes us financially rich. But it does not make us abundant.

Scarcity mindset has two main aspects: the belief that wealth and opportunity are limited and the innate fear that you will never have enough (Covey, 2020). This translates into a day-to-day existence of obsessing about what we do not have instead of valuing what we do have. We measure our worth according to the shortfall in reaching an assumed higher point (glass half empty). We pay little attention to appreciating how much we have achieved towards that higher goal. We judge ourselves not on where we have reached, but on how far we still have to go.

So, how does this show up in the workplace? We resent the success of others. When others get a salary rise, promotion, or bonus, we see this as being at our own expense rather than celebrating their success. We criticize others for mistakes or failure rather than complimenting them on their contributions or effort. We look for others to blame instead of stepping up to accept responsibility for our part. We measure ourselves according to how well we perceive others are doing. We tell ourselves that we are better than them. And we stay in this constant imagined competition with others in the absence of any other positive motivation to achieve.

By focusing on being the best, we lose sight of being our own highest self.

In doing so, we limit ourselves. We measure our achievements by results. We pull all-nighters to show our clients we can overdeliver. We measure how well we negotiate by what we gain at the expense of others. We do not feel we are doing enough unless we are running on empty. Because success comes at a price, valued by the extent of our willingness to sacrifice ourselves or others. I highlight in Table 8.1 some key differences between scarcity mindset and abundance mindset. It is truly surprising that we choose to sit in scarcity mindset when abundance mindset is so freeing.

Table 8.1 Differences between scarcity mindset and abundance mindset

Scarcity mindset	Abundance mindset
See effort as transactional	See effort as transformational
Find accomplishment through entitlement	Find accomplishment through gratitude

Fear uncertainty	Embrace change
Secretly hope others fail	Contribute to the success of others
Hoard information and data	Stay open to learning opportunities
Sit in blame, criticism, and anger	Live in joy, adventure, and fun
Have unclear objectives and focus	Set challenging goals and life plans
Take credit	Take responsibility
See success as limited	See achievement as limitless

Abundance is limitless

I was encouraged from an early age to work hard. Like many other first-generation ethnic Indians living in the United Kingdom from the late 1960s onwards, deferred gratification became my best friend. I dared not revel in the hazy blush of a recent success. I would immediately knuckle down to earn more, gain more, and achieve even better results than before.

In fact, I think that many professionals are engineered to believe they cannot be rich and successful without hard work, sacrifice, and a long and painful struggle. We are uncomfortable with ease; it is beneath us to stoop to a level below difficult. We need to take the hard path to ensure that when we succeed, it is wholly and deeply deserved.

The 'law of attraction' is a New Thought belief that states we attract into our lives whatever we focus on. Whatever we give our energy and attention to is what will come back to us. If we are anxious, stressed, angry, resentful, or sad, that negative energy will repel positivity and surround us with more negative energy – pessimistic people, unfortunate events, and such like. You may have already noticed the law of attraction affecting your own life. Perhaps you have told yourself you are not good enough to get that new job; you are then plagued by this negative, mean talk during your interview, and low and behold, you are not invited back for a second interview.

The law of attraction teaches us about the power of manifestation. It tells us that our thoughts and feelings create our reality and what we choose to focus on is what we will manifest in our lives. It also teaches us about the power of magnetism. It tells us that everything that has come into our lives – people, events, opportunities – is a result of the energy that we have put into the world. Put simply, we attract what we are.

It follows, therefore, that if we focus on the limitless abundance of potential in ourselves, we will automatically attract more positivity, opportunity, and success in our lives. Possibilities and options will flow as a direct result of us applying abundant thinking. If we tell ourselves in a job interview that 'this job *is* mine', we are exponentially increasing the likelihood that we will be offered the job.

Letting our past limit our future selves

What is it that holds us back from embracing the principle of unlimited abundance?

People, events, cultural background, and other environmental factors influence us from birth. Many influences have been positive. Some have not. We may have suffered harm, trauma, betrayal, or other wounds. All of these can make an indelible imprint on us and change the way we think, feel, and behave in life and work. These are the limitations of our past that wound our souls.

E.M. Forster describes such wounded souls as 'vast armies of the benighted' who have yielded to the enemy within (1995: 143). Gallwey (2001) alludes to working wounded, who, after years of silencing inner burdens, sacrifice, or struggles, begin to crack. Disconnection, discomfort, and loss of self start to show up on the surface in interactions, communications, and body language.

Benson (no date) adopts the analogy of an iceberg to illustrate the tension at surface level. What you often see above surface level is an outburst of anger or frustration. These are negative expressions of deeper inner disturbances that fester under surface level and show up reactively in unexpected and unrelated events. For example, a trainee supervisor, LC, was a calm and introverted partner with an enormous capacity for absorbing deal pressure and stress. Front of house – in meetings and in public – nothing could disarm her. No client demand was too great. In the privacy of her office, however, LC would unleash her wrath unexpectedly. On returning from a meeting that did not go her way or after a call with a client where she was not heard, she would calmy close her office door then unrestrainedly kick her bin until it was bashed in. To her clients, she was 'the swan'. To her colleagues, she was 'the bin kicker'.

Hendricks believes that there are four hidden barriers that hold us back from entering our 'zone of genius': feeling fundamentally flawed, being disloyal or abandoned, believing success brings greater burden, and fear of outshining (2009, pp. 45–56). The most common self-limiting core beliefs that I come across in helping coaching clients to change mindset are the inner judge ('I am flawed'), the inner critic ('I am unworthy'), the shameful one ('My needs do not matter'), and the unloveable one ('I am not enough'). By understanding the trance of unworthiness caused by these self-limiting core beliefs, we can start to notice the actual impact the beliefs have on us in our choices and decisions in the present.

At first, we may turn our self-limiting beliefs onto ourselves. We submerge our feelings and pour ourselves into the 'work hard, play hard' lifestyle. When this continues for a prolonged period and we reach our limits of tolerance, we can start to act out in moments of rage, anger, or frustration (like the bin kicker). Over time, we can also turn these wounds on others. We externalize our feelings and shift our focus to blaming, criticizing, and judging others. We obsess about how their ability or inability affects our progress and success. And over time, this fixation on others turns into resentment. Resentment for what we sacrifice, suffer, or bear in the present – and expectation that others should suffer in the same way too. Resentment for what others appear to be achieving or gaining – attention, promotion, recognition. As if what they are recognized for automatically subtracts from our own self-worth. Think about that for a moment. That someone else's success somehow automatically deducts from our own!

Tolle (2004) calls it our 'pain-body'. He uses this term to describe the accumulation of painful life experiences that we did not fully face and accept in the moment they arose. It leaves behind energy in the form of negative emotional pain, a mass of old negative emotion wrapped up inside. It is a familiar hurt inside us, a go-to place where negative emotions – sadness, fear, guilt, anger – are triggered. A default place of negative thought pattern that turns into a familiar place of retreat. It becomes our 'safe space', a place of comfort, even though it engulfs us in negative emotion and pain. The place we go to self-soothe is the place that feeds the exact negative emotion that we are seeking to avoid. And the pain-body simply grows (Tolle, 2004).

What has happened to us in the past can affect us in the present and in the future. But we can control how it influences us and our futures. Accepting ourselves for who we are is like giving ourselves a blank canvas. We can choose to step up and paint misery or step up and paint joy. Our futures lie in our own hands.

Detaching ourselves from results

I felt on top of my game. I had the highly coveted role, title, salary, benefits, and platform for success. I was prominent in the sector, multi-award winning, well recognized by industry press. However, I felt deeply unfulfilled. In fact, empty. Because I was aware that I was not walking my true path. I was walking the path of my ego but not being true to who I really am. I was aware that deeper fulfilment in life comes from greater service to others, and yet the person I was serving most in my life was me. What spurred me to take a radical change in direction, to relinquish control of results and turn instead to being in search of purpose? Belief. Belief in myself.

The law of attraction says that only when you truly detach from control over what you want are you free to attract what is destined for you. It is a lesson in letting go of results. When we fear uncertainty, change, or the unknown, our instincts tell us to hang on tight to what we have. In fact, we should do the opposite; we must create space between ourselves and whatever unknown is ahead of us. We should focus on that space, recognize it, embrace it, and be 100% comfortable with what it is – good and bad. Tolle puts it beautifully: 'When you become comfortable with uncertainty, infinite possibilities open up in your life' (2016, pp. 274–275).

The hardest part of letting go is the feeling of loss of control. We use control as a replacement for belief in ourselves and others. Why leave things to chance when we can control our steps to guaranteed success?

Only when we learn how to detach from control over results do we truly step into the arena of bounteous opportunities and possibilities. Returning to the example of me, I needed to let go of focusing only on financial targets, my bonus, and what others thought of me. I had to focus on my core capabilities, mindset, and behaviour, and believe that, no matter what, I would find a path of greater fulfilment. I needed to throw my arms in the air and proclaim: 'I don't care where my purpose takes me. I just want to know how it feels.'

The greatest courage of all is to know that success will be what you learn from embracing uncertainty.

Chapter 9

Shifting mindset from results to impact

Shifting focus from what we have achieved to connecting to a higher purpose means relinquishing our preoccupation with results. In its place, we focus simply on the process of change from fixed mindset to performance as learning. In doing so, we open our hearts to accepting that with risk comes greater reward.

What fixed mindset looks like

A results-focused lawyer is invariably in fixed mindset.

The core belief of someone who is sitting in fixed mindset is that their personal traits – intelligence, personality, moral character – are fixed. This creates urgency to continually prove themselves, using every opportunity to demonstrate their qualities in abundance. Dwek observes that the scariest thought for those in fixed mindset is the possibility of being ordinary, and this leads to their need for constant validation (2017, p. 30). When results are what demonstrate their success, they feel a sense of superiority, because the results mean their fixed traits are better than the fixed traits of other people (Dwek, 2017, p. 30). The better results they achieve, the more superior they feel (and the deeper entrenched they are in fixed mindset).

Fixed mindset sufferers fear failure because the experience of failure is transformed in their minds to an identity ('I am a failure'). They therefore avoid unnecessary risk of failure, such as opportunities for change. They become inflexible in the face of change. In extreme cases, they avoid change entirely ('I am what I am'). They also tend to display low emotional intelligence and shy away from self-scrutiny. They will not seek feedback on their skills or qualities in case comments fall short of their expectations. They can also fall easily into stances of judgement, blame, and criticism of others to detract from closer scrutiny of themselves (Dwek, 2017).

It is interesting to understand the impact that sitting in fixed mindset has on our ability to lead others. Fixed mindset sufferers often avoid conflict. Rather than tackle a problem head on, they will ask others to confront it so that they can avoid their fixed traits being questioned. They can feel threatened by the success of others and uncomfortable with recognition bestowed on others, thinking it detracts from their own sense of worth. They therefore pour energy into activities that recognize their own efforts rather than the efforts or successes of others. Most significantly, they are risk-averse, sitting in fear of potential failure. If they assume responsibility for a task with unclear or uncertain outcomes and fail, this translates, in their minds, to them being failures.

Unfortunately for us, law firms are full of fixed mindset sufferers. When the criterion for our success is singularly set at financial results, we are not incentivized or motivated to innovate, create, or experiment. We just need to take the shortest route possible to delivering maximum results. There is no room for risk; we do just enough to secure the intended results. When law firms measure success purely in terms of revenues and profits per equity partner and profits continue to rise, there is no urgency to change. There is no need to measure the negative impact of micromanagement, inflexibility, and incessant focus on team performance and productivity, or to address the opportunity costs of fixed mindset. The fixed mindset sufferers continue to sit in that mindset, counting their winnings.

What holds us back

Based on my own experience with colleagues, peers, and coaching clients, there are some fundamental barriers that prevent us from tackling the problem of fixed mindset:

- *Lack of urgency* – 'If I am making so much money from achieving these results, I do not need to change. I just need to stick at it for a few more years.'
- *Pursuit of perfection* – 'I must achieve perfection in everything I do. Nothing is good enough so if I strive for even better results next year, I will be even more perfect.' This translates, at individual level, to 'I must meet my greatest expectations of myself – at whatever cost.' (For details on letting go of perfection, refer to Chapter 7.)
- *Search for approval* – 'I need recognition in order to feed my self-worth. Demonstrating success through financial results attracts the approval I crave. I cannot

risk indulging in activities that may not lead to such recognition.'

- *Hunger for control* – 'I have an insatiable need for control of everyone and everything. I must have complete autonomy with no interference in my decision-making, and control over outcomes. Mobilizing and driving my team to achieve tangible results provides a satisfying level of control.'
- *Preoccupation with pain* – 'I must take the hard path. Rewards do not come without sacrifice. I cannot prove myself unless I have pushed myself to the limit and have some battle scars to show for my efforts.'

In each case, we are fixating on results (a function of our egos) as a measure of our success. Successful results feed our egos. We become obsessed with feeding ourselves this way, not fully appreciating how and when this stops serving us and those around us (we discuss ego in greater detail in Chapter 4). We stay squarely in our comfort zones to safeguard our egos and our positions. In an increasingly globalized world of disruptive change, however, success is about stretching ourselves beyond what is immediately comfortable and breaking into new frontiers. Failure is staying the same and not reaching for more.

What we require here is to acknowledge the limiting impact fixed mindset has on us and our ability to move forward. Only when we drop the attachment to results and replace this with a freeing, positive belief in improvement can we step into the arena of change and move towards achieving our highest potential.

What frees us

RJ, a salaried partner in a regional law firm, came to me for coaching support. 'It's like I'm in a trench', he said. 'The sides are so high I just can't see a way out.' He continued: 'I'm having a good year so far, so if I just keep my head down and power through, I should be okay. I have my partner sabbatical in three years in any case. I just need to hold on until then.'

RJ was firmly stuck in a fixed mindset. As our work together progressed, it became clear that the barricades RJ felt around him were in fact barriers to change that he himself was creating. 'I want to retire at 55.' 'I've promised the family a second home in the south of France.' RJ is not alone. I often see successful professionals becoming obsessed with maintaining their results for fear of what they might lose if they even think about changing what they do or how they do it. They fear losing what they have should they pursue the unknown.

But we do not dig out a trench by digging in. Only if we look up and connect to higher belief in ourselves are we propelled forward to make changes. Only if we dare to believe that we can be more, have more, and feel more do we connect to a motivation to rise up.

RJ and I worked on identifying and releasing the self-limiting beliefs entrenched in his fixed mindset thinking. We replaced the self-limiting beliefs he held regarding financial obligations with more freeing beliefs regarding his future. Through this process, we uncovered that he would be happy to continue working beyond the age of 55 if he were freed from the shackles of BigLaw and doing work he actually enjoyed, for clients he actually liked. We explored RJ's curiosity for NewLaw and passion for autonomy and flexibility in the deals he does and clients he serves. Soon enough, he was on that fulfilling path of change from BigLaw to NewLaw.

We lift ourselves out of a trench by visualizing what is on the other side. It is belief in the greater value we can gain that creates the motivation to climb up and over the top. Connecting to beliefs that free us will take us to places far beyond our present expectations.

Moving into growth mindset

In my own journey from doing high performance to being a conscious lawyer, shifting from fixed mindset was an essential early step. I was not aware of the impact of my fixed mindset ways until I started to submerge my ego (we discuss submerging ego in Chapter 7). When I turned my attention to seeking feedback from my colleagues on how they actually perceived me, I started to understand the power of going in search of greater learning and growth. I realized that learning would ease the path to change.

Growth mindset is based on the fundamental belief that our qualities can be cultivated by our efforts and strategies, and with support from others (Dwek, 2017, p. 7). Improvement comes through application and experience. Everyone has potential. It is effort that converts potential into ability and ability into achievement (refer to Figure 9.1).

We are in growth mindset when we see performance as learning and achievement as growth.

Figure 9.1 Effort converts potential to achievement

Throughout my own transformative journey, the rationale for my choices changed from 'What's in it for me?' to 'What will I learn?' If I suffered a setback, I would not feel defeated, imagining that someone else had gained from what I had lost. Instead, I considered it a deliberate bend in the path for me to appreciate and discover. And I would persist through it, sitting in the discomfort of it and knowing that this too shall pass.

By switching my focus from what I have to the journey of learning, my efforts became about being on a path to mastery. The learning became nourishment enough. I became thirsty for knowledge and greater understanding. I would actively seek feedback and act on it. The greatest difference from the fixed mindset I once held was that I found inspiration in the success of others. I no longer saw others as competition, but rather as potential enhancers of my own success (the difference between scarcity mindset and abundance mindset is discussed in Chapter 8).

Shifting to growth mindset is a constant process, difficult to lock in. Dwek explains that we tend to hold onto fixed mindset as it serves us well for so long (2017, p. 234). It helps us form a strong identity in terms of who we are (smart) and what we want to be (successful). It provides us with an instant formula for self-esteem and a path to financial security.

As lawyers, fixed mindset creates a convincing identity – competent, professional, ambitious – which becomes synonymous with who we are. Mindset change asks us to let go of this ego-self with which we so strongly identify. It is especially difficult to replace it with a mindset that tells us to embrace all that is threatening – challenge, criticism, setbacks.

When I was first going through the process of shifting from fixed mindset, it was incredibly unsettling. I lost my sense of self completely. I asked myself: 'Who am I if I am not "the general"?' Giving up on attachment to my old self meant losing my connection to my essential self. I felt fear I would not be my essential self anymore, as if my fixed mindset gave me my ambition, edge, and individuality. My greatest fear of all was that I would be 'ordinary'.

What helped me was following the advice of Dwek. She offers a four-step process for moving into growth mindset (2017, pp. 254–262). I summarize my experience of this process in Table 9.1; this is an ongoing process for me every day.

Table 9.1 How to move from fixed mindset to growth mindset

Steps		The experience
1	Embrace your fixed mindset	I put to one side any shame and judgement for having a fixed mindset. We all suffer from fixed mindset, and we need to be compassionate with ourselves in embracing how it has served, and can continue to serve, us in life.

2	Become aware of your fixed mindset triggers	I observe when my fixed mindset persona shows up. I notice, without judgement, what is happening inside my body when my fixed mindset is triggered – what negative feelings and emotions show up and how I respond.
3	Give your fixed mindset persona a name	By naming my fixed mindset persona, I am able to better acquaint myself with it, personalize it, and see it with greater perspective and compassion for myself. I have named mine 'Thatcher'.
4	Educate it	I have become open to going on a journey with my fixed mindset when it shows up. I greet it warmly, converse with it, and tell it what I am choosing to do and the benefit that will bring. I ask it to come along with me on a journey of discovery.

Moving into growth mindset is not about rejecting or suppressing fixed mindset. It is accepting that the two can coexist inside us. Over time, we switch our default mindset from the belief that we have innate talent to the belief we have capacity to learn.

Believing in impact

The common concern I hear from coaching clients – predominantly senior lawyers in demanding law firm and in-house roles – is that they are victims of their own success. They describe themselves as spinning too many plates that are becoming increasingly harder to maintain. They come to me seeking help with their leadership brands, their business cases for partnership, or how to find the elusive work–life balance. Pretty early on in our coaching journey, we find that what they are in search of is, in fact, the answer to the question 'What do I want?'

Finding fulfilment in life and work does not happen by manipulating external factors to meet our expectations. What happens to us as our success grows is that our expectations of ourselves grow too, until nothing is ever enough. Fulfilment comes from living life consciously – without ego – and making deliberate choices and decisions that align with what we want in the moment of now. Moving into growth mindset – where performance is learning – means accepting change must happen. We measure that change by the impact we have on the people around us.

As we evolve through the hierarchy of needs (Maslow, 1943) from meeting basic needs of safety and security to meeting psychological needs of community and relationships, we start to experience how our impact on other people has far greater prospects for delivering positive outcomes. Returning for a moment to Maxwell's (2013) five levels of leadership (discussed in Chapter 1), the shift from Level 3 (production) to Level 4 (people development) comes with a commitment to focusing on cultivating people more than on driving results. Our objective becomes delivering high performance results by developing the people around us so that they fulfil their highest potential. We shift focus from what we achieve to long-term investment in the impact of others – in other words, purpose over profits (this is discussed in greater detail in Chapter 13).

Workplaces are increasingly committing to create 'learning organizations' and 'knowledge economies'. This shift in focus acknowledges that working to produce immediate results is of limited value unless the primary objective of performance is to grow capability to improve future outcomes. Put simply, getting short-term results is of little value unless learning occurs in that process. Any focus purely on performance now is at the expense of greater knowledge, growth, and achievement in the future. This means performance criteria must broaden to measure behavioural competency, using indicators such as contribution to innovation, creativity, knowledge growth, and learning. Workplaces must rethink their attitudes to risk, shift from fearing and avoiding risk to embracing potential gains from experimentation and fresh thinking.

My daughter taught me this when she was eight years old. She was climbing a tree and had done well to navigate a complicated web of branches but reached the point of no return. She paused to consider her options: (a) take what she had achieved as a win and come back down or (b) take a blind leap of faith onto a branch some distance from where she was perched. We exchanged ideas on these options, and I offered her words of caution. 'The leap would be a brave move, my darling,' I said, 'but comes with a chance you'll miss your grasp and fall.' 'Yes,' she said, 'but that means there's a chance I will not.' And she leapt.

When we open our hearts to accept that risk brings with it a chance of greater reward, we allow change to happen.

Chapter 10
Choosing greater impact

When we accept that we can have greater impact, we give ourselves permission to allow orderly change to proceed. We connect to our visions for the impact we want to have in the world. We surrender to the process of effort and improvement. Most of all, we see making mistakes as our greatest opportunity for learning.

Going first in search of purpose

When I was contemplating a change in career direction from general counsel to law firm COO, I was clear in my head about what I *did not want*. Where I struggled was answering the question 'What do I want?' I had to connect to something much higher than what my strengths are and what I enjoy doing. I had to ask myself at fundamental level, 'What is it that I do that will allow me to contribute at my highest level of value?' I had to go in search of my purpose in life.

McKeown considers that the route to achieving greater fulfilment in work and life is to shift focus from 'having it all' to dedicating our energies to only those activities that make the highest contribution to things that really matter to us (2014, p. 157). The journey I embarked on was neither easy nor linear. I had to dig deep into my vision of my future – both professional and personal – and my values and passions in life. I had to uncover for myself what activities are so closely aligned with my values (we discuss alignment with values in Chapter 6) that they bring joy and fulfilment when I am fully ensconced in their practice. When I feel in flow (we discuss finding flow in Chapter 11) to such a degree that I lose myself fully and completely in the activity that is captivating my attention (Csikszentmihalyi, 2008). I realized through this process how much I love change – transformational change – and how passionate I am about working with others to radically change how legal services are delivered. This gave me the clarity to explore roles that would take me in the direction of my purpose in life: leading people into the future of law.

There are some practical steps you can take in the process of uncovering your purpose.

Create a vision for you

The simplest way to uncover what brings you joy, fulfilment, and happiness is to sit down and write a description of your perfect day. The act of free writing a series of events over the course of one day focuses your attention on what your heart tells you is happiness for you. Include all aspects of your relationships – family, friendships, colleagues – and your activities – work, sport, recreation. The exercise will help you uncover how you want your life to be, every day. For an exercise in creating a vision for you, visit www.kiranscarr.com/downloads.

Work out what is holding you back

Analyse what you are tolerating in your life that may be holding you back from living your best. Many aspects could be affecting your quality of life – career, money, relationships, physical health, environment. You may be applying too much emphasis on one aspect (maybe work) and not enough to others (maybe health and wellbeing). For an exercise on your wheel of life, visit www.kiranscarr.com/downloads. (For details of the importance of values alignment, refer to Chapter 6.)

Develop a strong sense of your *ikigai*

Ikigai – reason for being – is the practice of connecting the dots between your passion, vocation, profession, and mission (García and Miralles, 2017). By uncovering what fundamental core skills you have to offer to match what the world needs, you discover your ultimate purpose for being on this earth. This is a primary inner purpose of being rather than a secondary outer purpose of doing. In summary, ikigai lies at the centre of:

- *Your passion* – what you love doing. When you ask yourself what you loved to do when you were young, you can often uncover your truest passions in life. You can also examine what puts you in the state of flow (we discuss finding flow in Chapter 11).
- *Your vocation* – what you can contribute. When you are clear about where you make your highest contribution, you can identify where you can create your highest value. This requires you to focus on core competencies (problem-solving, creative thinking,

being a change agent) more than skills or strengths (negotiating, dealmaking).

- *Your profession* – what you can be paid for. You need to be clear on the roles that can generate active revenue or passive income for you in a sustainable and fulfilling way.
- *Your mission* – what matters to you. A fundamental part of establishing your purpose in life is to clearly articulate what you deeply care about. This is about articulating what you feel the world needs, what problems on this earth need solutions, and what you would change tomorrow if you had the divine power to do so.

By uncovering our purpose – our reason for being – we will connect to what we want. Our jobs or titles are not the sum of our intended contributions in life. There is a higher calling for each of us and the journey is to find it and live it wholeheartedly. For an exercise in finding your ikigai, visit www.kiranscarr.com/downloads.

Focusing on process, not destination

Making a shift in focus from what you have achieved to finding greater purpose is not about hustling your way to a destination. The path of transformation is a process of constant improvement and learning. It is about being present in the transition from doing high performance to being a conscious leader in your own life. It is a long journey that will take many twists and turns according to the choices you make along the way. It is about noticing changes as they happen, showing gratitude for progress and learning gained, and picking yourself up from mistakes or failures. It is about having a plan, or a series of plans, but being flexible, compassionate, and forgiving in how you deploy them. It is what you acquire along the way that allows the path to fulfilment to lead the way.

Through my own journey and that of many clients and colleagues I have worked with, I have learnt that a fundamental step in choosing greater impact is shifting attention from outcome to the process of transformation itself. We must detach ourselves from any concept of destination and simply embark on the journey of change. We must switch our measures of success from external markers to what is happening inside us. We must become aware of our behaviours, our responses, and how we feel. We must realize that the only things we can control are the choices we make in any given moment. And we must start to experiment and try new ways of dealing with situations. We must not judge the outcome, even if it is unintended.

Table 10.1 sets out what it looks like to shift from leadership as a destination to leadership as an ongoing process of change. Focusing on results and outcomes is doing leadership; conscious change as a process is being a leader in your own life. You may also wish to refer to Table 7.1, which locates these shifts to specific energy centres in your body.

Table 10.1 What it looks like to transfer attention from doing leadership to being a leader

From doing leadership	To being a leader
Being task orientated Focusing primarily on the destination and outcome through control of tasks and inputs	Focusing on the experience of now Focusing primarily on making yourself open to what is happening now to enable progress to flow
Delivering results Maximizing your input to achieve the highest output (scarcity mindset)	Unleashing untapped potential Freeing your thinking to consider unlimited possibilities and opportunities (abundance mindset)
Demonstrating power Harnessing your strength, pushing through hardship, overcoming obstacles, and making sacrifices	Showing heartfelt courage Opening your heart, embracing the unknown, opening up to vulnerabilities, and showing care and compassion
Labelling success Subscribing to the identity of success – title, salary, rewards, etc.	Recognizing achievement Seeing achievement in terms of learning and growth in your purpose and sense of self
Absorbing pressure Suffering in silence, submerging needs, being inflexible to change	Investing in self-care Nourishing your physical, emotional, mental, and spiritual needs
Relying on personal judgement Delivering results through competing, controlling, deciding, and telling	Seeking advice and input Influencing outcomes through seeking and deploying information, knowledge, expertise, and advice
Having a strong sense of self Living through the ego version of your self	Submerging ego Living through personal values and sense of self

The seven key areas of change are described below.

From being task orientated to focusing on the experience of now

When moving any deal or project forward, our default is to take a task-orientated approach – checklists, milestone dates, tracker documents, target dates. We drive results one push at a time. When we shift to focusing on greater impact, we keep attention on where we want to get to, but our primary focus is making ourselves open and available to enable the next steps to flow. To do that, we must stay at balcony view, aware of what is happening from an elevated position. Rather than staying on the dance floor, at operational level, we heighten our view and respond as and when needed to ensure any blockages or obstacles are cleared as progress is made. What is important to know here is that the learning is in experiencing the now as it occurs rather than fixating on the ultimate destination.

From delivering results to unleashing untapped potential

When we lead, we often think in terms of maximizing input to achieve the best output. But this is scarcity mindset in action (we discuss this in Chapter 8). We are approaching the situation from the perspective that we have limited resources available. Why not instead discharge the limiting assumption and replace it with a positive, freeing assumption – 'I have unlimited potential for making this a success' (we discuss freeing ourselves from limiting beliefs in Chapter 9). This unlocks what is subconsciously holding us back and enables us to change the question from 'What can I do with what I have?' to 'How can I make this happen?'

From demonstrating power to showing heartfelt courage

We associate achievement with strength – pushing on through, overcoming the hardest of obstacles, making sacrifices to get there. The result is that we close our hearts to the outside. This is very helpful as it protects us from harm. But it also stops us showing love, compassion, and care for ourselves and others. When we shift to focusing on greater impact, we open our hearts to what possibilities and opportunities may arise. It is scary to embrace the unknown in the vulnerable state of an open heart. But by showing courage rather than strength, we unleash the power we have inside to go beyond our own expectations of ourselves. We enter the realm of abundant self (connection to greater courage and compassion is discussed in detail in Chapter 7).

From labelling success to recognizing achievement

What often holds us back are the labels we have for ourselves (such as 'top biller' or 'equity partner'). What prevents us from taking the next step is not knowing what labels will replace them if we risk change. When we shift our attention from destination to process, we look for recognition based on the changes we achieve in ourselves and others. We applaud milestones achieved in our learning journeys and see these as completed rows in the rich tapestries that we are weaving for ourselves. We replace hierarchy with collaboration and inclusion, and achieve learning and progress through involvement and buy-in from those around us.

From absorbing pressure to investing in self-care

The more we are burdened with, the more we bear. Often in silence. If time pressure is upon us, the first thing we are willing to lose is attention to our own needs. And yet we cannot help others when we are running on an empty tank. In times of crisis, we stiffen our backs, hold our heads high, and biff on. Often, we only say no when we are broken. When we shift to focusing on greater impact, we focus every day on our self-care. It becomes the primary priority in our calendar – we schedule our lives around our self-care and not vice versa. We attune to our bodies and what they are telling us. We make time for meals as a ritual; we nourish mind and body not only by what we eat but through when and how we eat. We take care of our body as it is the only place we have to live.

From relying on personal judgement to seeking advice and input

Why is it the more experienced we are, the less inclined we are to ask questions? Surely we should be more confident to speak up and more curious to learn what others may think and know? We have learnt so much from others along the way, and yet we see it as weakness to be seen to not know something. When we shift to focusing on greater impact, we crave information, knowledge, and new learning from wherever we can get it. And this means we engage more with others for their ideas, perspectives, and connections. We accept we are human and do not know everything, and deploy the golden rule of any lawyer – if you don't know the answer, find someone who does.

From having a strong sense of self to submerging ego

It is important to have a strong leadership brand. People you lead need to understand who you are and what you stand for. It is equally important to put that brand into action by behaving in a way that is true to it (we discuss leadership brand in Chapter 5). That is authentic leadership. But there is often a fine line between living your brand through your ego-self and through your conscious-self (we discuss this in Chapter 7). If you find yourself struggling to keep up with the social media version of your life, you are living through your ego-self. If you make choices by behaving in a way that is aligned with your values, you are living according to your conscious-self (we discuss this in Chapter 6). When we shift our attention to process, our focus changes from what others might think to how we make others feel. Less ego, more humility.

Being a leader is a constant process of improvement. Building our impact as leaders never ends, because we evolve through life. With every effort to change comes a need to accept that mistakes will happen and that there is greater learning in that.

Being prepared to fail

KT is a senior partner and the sole female board member at an international law firm. She is also head of the global committee for diversity and inclusion. She was tasked with choosing a chief diversity and inclusion officer, a newly created board position, from a list of two preselected candidates. Both candidates were highly qualified; the main distinguishing factor was that one candidate, a man, had fulfilled a C-suite role previously, whilst the other candidate, a woman, had not.

KT is a conscious lawyer. She is a values-based leader who embraces the firm's corporate values in how she behaves and the decisions she makes (we discuss alignment with values in Chapter 6). She was aware that the female candidate did not have a proven track record of success as a C-suite leader. Nevertheless, she selected her for the role. The rationale for her decision? The opportunity to appoint another female board member was something that touched the core of her beliefs. As a purpose-driven leader who is passionate about making a difference, she knows that unless she herself appoints qualified female candidates into senior positions, there will not be substantive change to female board representation in the law firm. The mindset she adopted to make this choice? Growth mindset. KT is a leader who is prepared to experiment and take risks and learn from the consequences of doing so.

Part of adopting growth mindset is being open to a lifetime of learning. Learning comes in many shapes and forms, not least experimenting, making mistakes, and course correcting. Think about how we learn as junior lawyers – through trial and error. We are not expected to know how to draft a share and purchase agreement on day one. We start with a first draft and learn through feedback, revision, and practice. The bigger the challenges given to us, the more we are motivated to stretch and learn from what we do not know. Our commitment to improve comes with willingness to fail.

When we connect to our purpose, we connect to our higher journey of evolution and change. When we focus on process and not destination, change becomes inevitable. Our fear of what might be transforms into belief in unlimited reward.

Chapter 11

Focusing on experience every day

Surrendering to change is hard; it pushes us beyond our boundaries of comfort. When we achieve the state of 'flow' in our experiences every day, we feel enjoyment in the face of challenge. We become lost in the flow, which silences our inner demons of dissent. So, change becomes effortless.

Using flow to deliver outcomes

There is a general counsel, HS, who I admire greatly. She has an incredibly high-risk job overseeing a regulated financial services business and makes difficult choices every day. She does so with care, composure, and, above all, consistency. I once asked her how she manages it all with such gravitas and grace. She replied: 'I love what I do. When I'm at work, it's like I've come home to me.'

Csikszentmihalyi (2008) describes the concept of 'flow' as a feeling of enjoyment that appears at the boundary between boredom and anxiety, when challenges are balanced finely with a person's ability to act (refer to Figure 11.1).

For this blissful state to exist, a task must be challenging enough to require deep concentration to a degree that removes from our awareness the worries and frustrations of everyday life. As such, it is different from our unchallenging recreational activities, such as flicking through sports news or binge-watching a favourite Netflix series. What is key to flow is that attention is so concentrated that concern for the 'thinking' self disappears. We lose ourselves in the flow activity. When we emerge from the flow experience, we feel a deeper sense of self, a heightened level of completeness (Csikszentmihalyi, 2008).

Figure 11.1 The state of flow

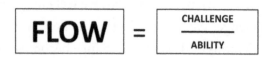

This optimal experience presents an end in itself; it is intrinsically rewarding. It operates as a self-contained activity, done not with the expectation of some future benefit but simply because the doing itself is the source of much enjoyment. The person who achieves flow pays attention to the activity for its own sake, without thought of progress or outcome (Csikszentmihalyi, 2008, p. 71). Contrast this with our state when we focus on results. Our attention is almost exclusively focused not on the activity itself but on achieving its consequences. We are in the state of drive, push, or hustle, almost always at the expense of learning and improvement.

I felt the difference between focus on results and attention to experience when writing this book. When I started the journey, I tackled it much as a lawyer would draft a contract. I put together a skeleton of headings and came up with a strict schedule of sections I would compete by stated deadlines. I laboured away for weeks, with enjoyment diminishing as fast as frustration grew. When it came to writing this chapter, I decided to practise what I was preaching and shifted my approach to one of flow. I dispensed with the section plan and instead grouped my writing into topics, the completion of which would give me a sense of accomplishment. I would tackle each topic only when I felt the urge to do so, at which times my concentration would be so intense that I would lose myself in the process. My attention was such that I was without distraction or worry for how I was doing and how I was performing. To paraphrase the words of Csikszentmihalyi, it was as if there was a perfect integration of my desire, my capability, and my inner joy, expressed in the creative action of writing (2008, p. 49). During these periods of enhanced creativity, the experience became so effortless and gratifying that time seemed altered; hours felt like minutes. My family would come knocking on my office door asking when I might appear again.

Gallwey refers to flow as 'Self 2 focus' (2001, p. 51). He describes it as a flow and rhythm to your actions that is inherently satisfying, where performance flows smoothly and effortlessly, allowing learning to take place naturally and spontaneously. He concludes that two core conditions must be present: sufficient safety and challenge (Gallwey, 2001, p. 53). Like Csikszentmihalyi (2008), he sees it as a balance between stress and boredom. Too much challenge and not enough safety will lead to stress; too little challenge and too much safety will lead to boredom (Gallwey, 2001, p. 53).

Achieving balance between stress and boredom has a direct impact on our overall awareness of our experiences. It has everything to do with getting the balance right between making the right choices in any given moment and stretching ourselves in aspects of our lives that are challenging enough to make us want more. As the bumper sticker says, 'Life begins at the edge of your comfort zone'.

It is the motivation to stretch beyond comfort that is essential to creating the flow experience. There are two types of motivation. There are tangible motivations, like a pay rise, promotion, or bonus. These commonly reward past efforts. Then there are intangible motivations, like creating a higher profile, leading a strategic project, or working for a new client, sector, or specialty. These recognize potential for future gain. It is these intangible rewards that connect us to the learning and growth that is the hallmark of the flow experience.

Csikszentmihalyi found in his studies that every flow activity provides a sense of discovery, a creative feeling of transporting the person into a new reality (2008, p. 74). It pushes the person to higher levels of performance. The joy of change is not seeking to reach a notional stage of transformed self. The joy derives from living every day of a learning experience that is so challenging and gratifying in itself that we are willing to do it for its own sake (Csikszentmihalyi, 2008, p. 74).

Table 11.1 is a description of how it feels to be in the state of flow. For an exercise in what puts you in flow, visit www.kiranscarr.com/downloads.

Table 11.1 How it feels to be in the state of flow

When I am in flow:
• I am dissolving my ego – my sense of self merges with what I am doing.

- I am transparent – I am not trying to be anyone other than who I am.
- I am challenging myself – I am doing things I would not normally try.
- I am following my intuition – I look for signs of what is not apparent on the surface.
- I am believing in myself – I know I am wise and listen to the wisdom that comes from within.
- I am silencing fear – I do not think of what might go wrong and trust completely in the process itself.

Change happens when we find the tipping point between challenge and ability to act. We know that we are stretching, but we are motivated to move forward because of the learning involved.

It is not that we *must* take the hard road. We are simply compelled to journey the road we are on.

All we have is the present moment

Being in flow experience is about making conscious choices about what we do and when and how we do it. Rather than focusing on task delivery according to relative urgency and demand, we must detach ourselves from outcome. We must let go of control and switch to being mindful only of the present moment.

We see each situation through our thinking minds, just as others see the same situation through their thinking minds. So, the same situation is always seen from different realities. What exists is the space between these perspectives. And in that space lies the now. The now is the point at which we must make choices about how to observe, decide, and respond.

There is no right or wrong. In the absence of judgement or blame, there is just a moment of choice. Gallwey calls it the 'inner game' – a state of nonjudgemental acknowledgement of things as they are (2001, p. 12). The ability to notice only what is in front of you and not wish it to be any different from how it is in that moment.

As explored in greater detail in Chapter 7, adopting mindfulness practices like sitting in stillness, breath work, and meditation will acquaint you with how it feels to be present in the moment. When we sit at peace and close our eyes, we can access a window into the vast arena of our inner consciousness. If, at first, you have difficulty sitting in silence or peace, you might benefit from some of the many online resources offering guided meditations, breathing exercises, and other relaxation techniques designed to teach how to access our inner beings. When we allow ourselves access to the stillness that lies within, we access a source of wisdom, power, and courage that we learn to trust in our choices day to day.

When we discover the power of being present in the now, we do not look to external sources to guide our choices. We simply look inside ourselves for the wisest answers of all.

Letting our thinking get in the way

Like many, I have an inner critic. I call him 'Bob'. He usually surfaces when I am at my strongest and most powerful – say, at a board meeting. Every time I speak up, he will tell me to be quiet. 'Who do you think you are?' he will say. 'You sound ridiculous. Why did you put it like that? They'll think you don't know what you're talking about!' In the early days, I used to listen to him and silence myself. If I needed to speak up, I would do so with little conviction in my voice. And my judgement would be impaired. It was only after I discovered mindfulness and the practice of meditation that I learnt I am not my thoughts. The words of Bob are not who I am. And by silencing his words – extinguishing them from my mind through mindful practice – I would create space to connect to the power inside me to speak up and shine.

Gallwey refers to our critical inner dialogue as our 'Self 1' (2001, p. 7). Self 1 describes the state of allowing our thinking to interfere with our performance and learning. The interference that we hear is the culmination of external voices from our past – critical family members, poor role models, dark triad bosses – that we have subconsciously incorporated into our identity. These voices set the highest of expectations, issue unreasonable demands or instructions, and attempt to hijack our present reality. If we listen to them often and long enough, they slowly erode our sense of wholeness, shatter our confidence, and undermine our ability to perform.

You can connect to your inner critic at any time. Simply close your eyes and it may well spring up to greet you. Notice the voices that appear in your head and speak to you. There may be one dominant voice, a saboteur, reminding you that you are unworthy or that you are not enough. There may be a series of whispers that culminate in an overall sense that you do not belong (imposter syndrome). The impact is the same: the critical inner dialogue is trying to sabotage who you really are – your strengths, your abilities, your values. It is trying to use its thunderous power to extinguish your 'Self 2' (Gallwey, 2001, p. 7).

Gallwey's Self 2 is the self we enjoyed as a young child. It embodies all the inherent potential we are born with, including all our current and future capabilities. It also embodies our innate ability to learn and grow any of these inherent capacities. Our strongest performance happens when Self 1's voice is silenced and Self 2 is allowed to operate undisturbed. Silencing Self 1 and nourishing the natural desires of Self 2 builds stability in being and creates a stronger sense of purpose and fulfilment (Gallwey, 2001).

In silencing Self 1, you cannot use resistance, force, or command. The more you seek to control Self 1, the more you feed it and the stronger it becomes. Instead, practise noticing Self 1, choosing to ignore it, and consciously choosing Self 2. In silencing Self 1 and selecting Self 2, you must intentionally acknowledge the needs and desires of Self 2 and allow it to express itself fully. Table 11.2 shows how we can select Self 2 by silencing Self 1.

Table 11.2 Silencing Self 1 and selecting Self 2

	Self 1	Self 2
What it is	Your critical inner dialogue	Who you are
What it does	Dominates your thinking	Powers your desires
How to approach it	Notice it. See it for what it is. Let it settle.	Connect to it. Embrace it. Align your behaviour to honour it.

The key here is to see the Self 1 thoughts for what they are, observe them, and let them rest. Create space for them. Be aware of them at source without wishing they were different.

Watch them float to the bottom of your conscious mind. Do not judge yourself for having them; just watch them and let them go. Know that they are just thoughts, and they are not who you are. Once the mental chatter has subsided, you are ready to turn towards your feelings. Allow your body to feel where you are and what you are doing, without letting your thinking mind take the feeling and make it something it is not. Sit in that feeling and let it take over your self. When you select Self 2, you are powered by your consciousness – a force that you will soon learn to trust more than your head.

GA is a general counsel who, over time, has taught herself how to choose Self 2 in the present moment. GA was presenting at a board meeting when a board member abruptly interrupted to make a point that GA was about to address. Her immediate reaction was anger, but she said nothing. Her inner critic had popped up to say: 'Serves you right. You aren't articulate enough.' In times gone by, she would have strongly reacted by talking over the board member to complete her point. On this occasion, she selected Self 2; she let her feelings be felt. Instead of moving from thoughts to action, she moved from thoughts to feelings. She let her body feel the anger surface and held a space for those feelings. In that space of feelings, GA chose another response. A response that came from a stronger, more reliable source of power – her intuition.

When the meeting recessed, GA took the board member aside in private. She asked him whether he was aware that he had interrupted her. 'I have no idea what you are talking about', he said. Unperturbed, she explained that the interruption during her presentation had made her feel disrespected in her thinking and her voice. 'In future meetings,' she said 'if you can wait until I finish before you speak, I will make sure I do the same when you speak.'

Where is the inner critic now?

When we connect to our inner game – our flow – we realize that what we crave is not simply balance in life and work. What we are really in search of is a state of being that is the tipping point between challenge and ability. When we sit in this state of constant fulfilment, with each act, we come closer to living a life of deep purpose.

When we have courage to let go of our attachment to results, we free ourselves to discover the potential that lies within. Rather than feed our ego-selves, we silence our inner critics and start the journey of change through challenging ourselves to grow. In doing so, we dedicate our efforts to converting our potential for impact to actual impact on other people. Abundance flows.

Leap II in a nutshell

- When we use high performance results as our primary criterion for success, we are focused on being the best (competition) rather than achieving our highest self (potential). This comes from a scarcity mindset. We pay little attention to how much we have and judge ourselves according to what we do not have.

- In fact, success is abundant. When we subscribe to abundance thinking, we become comfortable with uncertainty and our potential becomes limitless. We are no longer held back by our attachment to results.

- Results-focused lawyers are invariably in fixed mindset; they believe their abilities are static. Their egos prevent them from tackling the issue that their fixed mindset is limiting them. As their success grows, they become preoccupied with achieving even greater results to demonstrate that their innate abilities are superior.

- Growth mindset is based on the fundamental belief that everyone can improve through application and experience. Only when we drop our attachment to results and replace it with a freeing, positive belief in human ability to improve can we step into the arena of leading through change.

- Adopting growth mindset means shifting our focus from results to people. We commit to a longer-term investment in developing the people around us to fulfil their highest potential. We choose purpose over profits.

- When we go in search of purpose – our reason for being – we connect to what we want in life and work. We realize that there is a higher calling for us as leaders, and the journey is to find it and live it wholeheartedly.

- Making a shift from what we have achieved to finding greater purpose is a process, not a destination. It is an ongoing process of change from doing leadership to being a leader in our own life. The process never ends, because we transform through a lifetime of learning. With every effort to change comes a need to accept that mistakes will happen and that there is greater learning in that.

- Surrendering to change is hard; it pushes us beyond our boundaries of comfort. When we achieve the state of 'flow', however, we feel enjoyment in the face of the experience of change, because we find the tipping point between challenge and ability. Experiencing change becomes so satisfying that it proceeds without need for any external motivation.

- We become so lost in our flow that our inner critic – Self 1 – is silenced. When we select what we desire – Self 2 – in the absence of fear, judgement, or doubt, change becomes effortless.

- When we choose to be in a state of constant performance as learning, we start living lives of deeper fulfilment and purpose that connect us to our potential for greater impact.

LEAP III:

Relate to the people around you

It does not serve to bear weight so great
You become brittle and snap.

To live in leadership is
To bend, to crouch, to lean, to flex.

Consider the lilies of the field,
They do not toil.

Neither do they spin.

They fold, they sway, they bow,
To reveal their beauty
Their vulnerability, their brilliance, their
divine power.

When faced with challenge, conflict,
or hardship,
Do not stiffen with resolve.

Bend and others will move towards you.

Chapter 12

Why impact on people matters

Leap II is a lesson in shifting focus from performing for results to experiencing learning every day. In Leap III, we fully connect to our limitless potential to have greater impact in leading change. We embark on the journey of discovering how we can step back to create the optimum environment for the people around us to transform their potential into achievement.

Awareness of impact

MH worked in a high-profile in-house legal team. The general counsel to whom she reported was a leading figure in the in-house community and a prominent advocate for female leadership. MH came to me for coaching support as she was ready for a new role. 'I'm on tenterhooks all the time', she said. 'We have so much going on – governance changes, digital transformation projects, and new businesses being acquired – and my boss just expects us to get it done. I'm really at breaking point.'

What followed was an account of bigger picture issues relating to this general counsel's high expectations of her team. MH described how the team would fear admitting to delays or problems in case of criticism or blame. Many in the team had become defensive, deflective of responsibility, or simply noncommittal in the face of inquiry. Team members were often off sick and would gossip and complain about their colleagues. Team attrition was also an issue. Most endured the environment for a couple of years then quit. Some continued to endure, mentally quitting but staying in their role. Their impact left a deeper imprint on an already demoralized team dynamic. The interesting point to note is that based on the general counsel's strong public brand, the team did not have any problem recruiting fresh top talent. But the cost of this general counsel's leadership style was high. The cost was how she made people feel.

Every comment, action, and choice we make has impact. Felt in a moment, these can have lasting effect even after the event has long passed. I recall clearly MH's words when she described being publicly reprimanded by her boss: 'I do not even remember what she said to me, but I will never forget the shame I felt inside.' After an event is forgotten in our conscious minds, we can still feel, etched in our bodies, the scars of bad behaviour. Those scars have an impact on us in the future, on how we feel about ourselves and others.

When we fail to lead ourselves, our behaviour can leave a negative imprint on the people around us – our behaviour diminishes others.

Impact on people

What happens when a leader fails to lead themselves? When we consider the impact of poor leadership, common themes arise. Team members feel:

- *Disempowered* – they describe feeling blocked, underutilized, disenfranchised, and held back.
- *Disengaged* – they – high performers, particularly – switch off if they are limited to focused goals which do not stretch or challenge them.
- *Demotivated* – in the absence of connection to higher purpose, they lose sight of what is important or necessary.
- *Dehumanized* – they feel overcontrolled to the extent they feel like a cog in a wheel.

How does this affect employees and the businesses they serve in the longer term? The result is:

- *Absence of accountability* – without accountability, trust is entirely eroded. No one steps up and everyone plays safe.
- *Absence of responsibility* – in a culture of fear, blame, or overbearing criticism, team members avoid or deflect responsibility. People start to pass the buck in fear of making a mistake.
- *Low commitment* – team members do only what is required to achieve the intended result. There is no space for experimentation, creativity, or innovation.
- *Low fulfilment* – the workforce becomes unsustainable. A revolving recruitment door emerges as many quit rather than address the underlying issue of poor leadership.
- *A race to the bottom* – low engagement encourages a culture of 'acceptable' performance. In the absence of anything to reach for, mediocrity sets in.

In traditional law firms and corporate legal departments focused on delivering short-term results, the opportunity cost of poor leadership is relatively low. Revenues and profits per equity partner remain buoyant. Lawyer churn is viewed as a necessary by-product of leading high performance. In these technologically disruptive times, in which we must do more with less, create innovative solutions, and motivate a new generation of workforce, poor leadership must be tackled. As discussed in Chapter 2, in these turbulent times of global challenge, we all must acquire new leadership behaviours that focus on our impact on people in the workplace.

The cost of impact

A recent report (Brassey et al., 2022) presents some staggering correlations between toxic workplace behaviour and rates of employee burnout and attrition. Toxic workplace behaviour describes interpersonal behaviour that leads to employees feeling unvalued, belittled, or unsafe, such as unfair or demeaning treatment, noninclusive behaviour, sabotage, cut-throat competition, abusive management, and unethical behaviour of colleagues. In all 15 countries in Brassey et al.'s (2022) study, and across all aspects assessed, toxic workplace behaviour was found to be the biggest predictor of burnout symptoms and intent to leave. Other findings from the study include the following:

- One in four employees reported having experienced high rates of toxic behaviour.

- Employees who reported experiencing high levels of toxic workplace behaviour were eight times more likely to experience burnout symptoms.
- Employees reporting burnout symptoms were six times more likely to register an intent to leave within three to six months of assessment.

The authors conclude that conservative estimates of the cost of replacing employees range from one half to two times annual salary. Add to this the costs associated with the downward spiral of performance arising from burnout – including low engagement, lost commitment to the organization, lost productivity, and more sick pay (Brassey et al., 2022, pp. 7–8) – and that is costly impact.

GBS Corporate Training (2017), citing Smart CEO and DDI, provides estimates on the impact of poor leadership:

- Organizations operate with an estimated 5–10% productivity 'drag' arising from poor leadership.
- Suboptimal leadership practices cost the typical organization as much as 7% of their total annual revenue.
- Between 9% and 32% of an organization's voluntary attrition can be avoided through better leadership skills.
- Better leadership can lead to a 1.5% increase in revenue growth.
- A bad leader costs a company more than USD 126,000 annually due to lower productivity, reduced revenue, and employee discord.

In any organization facing challenge and where pressure, stress, and uncertainty affect how we behave every day, the cost of failing to change the way we lead is simply too high.

Shifting to sphere of influence

As discussed in Chapter 2, law firms and corporate legal departments are feeling increased pressure to respond to internal and external factors affecting their service delivery. This degree of disruption requires leaders to develop enhanced skills in bringing people together to create new client offerings, reinvent business models, and experiment with resourcing practices. The leader of change must mobilize teams to collaborate and innovate to deliver legal services differently.

When we shift our focus from achieving results to converting potential, we are shifting our attention to how we can attract opportunities and transform them from options to reality. We are not interested in attracting unfocused possibilities. We shift to those people who have potential to contribute most to our value. To paraphrase McKeown, we take on the role of editor in our lives, and in leadership, in order to focus only on the essential few who will add to our level of contribution (2014, p. 156).

The groups who contribute most to our value – our sphere of influence – are found in among key stakeholders. These are the essential few who play a specific role in contributing to our opportunities now and in the future. They are:

- *internal clients* – primary stakeholders within your organization;

- *external clients* – shareholders, suppliers, customers, and adviser clients;
- *partners and intermediaries* – third-party collaborators who can complement your contribution; and
- *other contacts* – sector, industry, or market contacts, and past or present associators, such as alumni groups.

For an exercise on how to identify and manage your sphere of influence, visit www.kiranscarr.com/downloads.

When we shift our focus to how we can influence the contribution of our key stakeholders, we align our behaviour to influencing the achievement of potential in ourselves and those around us.

Harnessing potential

In Chapter 9, we note that effort converts potential to achievement. When we shift our focus from achieving results to converting potential in others, we are shifting our focus from tasks to people. We are throwing out the old rule book that says we must focus on the destination, and, in its place, we are choosing to focus on the process of interacting with our sphere of influence. Our day-to-day focus becomes about how we can deepen and strengthen our relationships with the people around us. We look at ways in which we can contribute to our value through partnership, collaboration, and mutual support.

We shift our focus from a state of doing to a state of being. How we achieve this is discussed in detail in Chapter 13. In simple terms, the focus is on the experience we have with each person we interact with in any given moment. Attention is given to where they are and what they may need from us. Our primary goal is to come away having nurtured growing relationships with them. The success criterion from each interaction is not the outcome from it but rather, the quality of the interaction. This is measured principally by the human-to-human connection we make through the following:

- the questions we ask;
- the interest we show;
- the ideas we generate;
- the common interests we discover; and
- the trust we build.

By prioritizing what others need through asking the right questions, being curious and explorative in a collaborative manner, and aligning our actions with what is agreed, we create a vibrant ecosystem of stakeholders that operates to contribute to greater success overall.

By humanizing our sphere of influence, we shift our focus from 'me' to 'us'. By putting our efforts towards how people experience who we are, we come closer to realizing the highest potential in ourselves and those around us.

Chapter 13

Being the conscious lawyer

When we measure our success by the impact we have on the people around us, we subscribe to a higher level of integrity as leaders. It marks a fundamental change in how we behave every day. We take conscious steps to connect people to their purpose. And we teach them how to lead themselves through change.

Choosing conscious leadership

The word 'conscious' implies being more thoughtful, more awake, and more intentional in our embrace of our roles and responsibilities. In terms of leadership, it means stepping up to a higher level of responsibility and integrity, which requires an inner journey of character development and personal transformation. It marks a deliberate choice to lead differently in pursuit of higher purpose (Mackey, McIntosh, and Phipps, 2020, p. xv).

Conscious leadership requires a shift from treating business as an opportunity to compete and win to committing to serve and uplift people and communities (Mackey, McIntosh, and Phipps, 2020, p. xix). When people are led by a conscious leader, it feels different. They are being led by a values-based people leader who is purpose driven and wants them to make their highest contributions. A conscious leader actively listens to what people have to say; they are interested in their points of view. We know that because the conscious leader shows interest in team members' goals and aspirations, and they ask questions. They are curious to hear team members' ideas and will explore their thinking with them. They create space around them in which their team members can be creative, open to learning, and challenge themselves. They give their undivided support and create an environment of experimentation and innovation. Ideas and options are discussed and allowed to evolve before they are assessed for viability. There is a no blame culture, which means judgement is left at the door and mistakes are seen as opportunities for learning.

Conscious leaders, at their core, understand that they can create greater impact in these changing times through fostering a culture of learning. They create a sense of collective purpose that engages and empowers people to focus on maximizing their contribution to the overall rather than just their parts. By connecting each person to the way in which they can contribute to a higher vision and purpose, conscious leaders unlock understanding of higher potential in people, which emboldens them to stretch beyond their immediate reach.

When we choose to be conscious leaders, we choose to embrace uncertainty and let the journey unfold.

Identifying a conscious lawyer

We can identify a conscious lawyer in three main ways.

Who they are

They are courageous enough to shift their attention from controlling high performance results to creating the optimum environment for the people around them to develop and grow. They are purpose driven, which means they prioritize long-term, sustainable reward over short-term profits. They are values based, meaning they align their behaviour with their core beliefs and will service the best interests of their organizations over their own personal gain. They adopt growth mindset and understand that leadership requires a lifetime of learning. They are curious about understanding different perspectives and are willing to course correct and make mistakes. They proactively encourage experimentation, ideation, and innovation. Above all, they embrace their humanness from their hearts; they show humility, empathy, and compassion for those around them.

What they focus on

Because they value impact on people over task completion, they shift focus from the destination to the process itself. They put trust in their strategic vision and dedicate attention to the path of learning that leads them to realizing their vision. The process is not simple or predictable, but rather a journey of course correcting and overcoming challenge. They use their strong communication skills and surround themselves with the best people in terms of expertise and input. They understand their limitless power to fulfil potential in others and focus on those individuals who can contribute to their highest value. They enable the essential few to contribute at their best.

How they behave

Their focus on the experience of learning means they dedicate attention to the impact their behaviour has on the people around them. Put simply, they focus on how they make people feel. Their role is to unleash people's unlimited potential to exceed their own expectations of what they can do and learn. This means creating the optimum environment for their teams to feel engaged and empowered. The conscious lawyer measures success in terms of the improvement, learning, and growth of the people around them.

From results to people

When we shift our focus from producing high performance results to leading people, we take deliberate steps to elevate our leadership from Level 3 (production) to Level 4 (people development) (Maxwell, 2013). (This concept is discussed in greater detail in Chapter 1.)

At Level 3 leadership (production), the leader is focused on managing processes to produce best results. This works well in stable environments where operations can be standardized and to some degree predicted. Cracks appear, however, as global challenges and the need for change arise. The emergence of increased competition, technological disruption, and generational shifts in the workplace has made the shift up to Level 4 leadership (people development) a prerequisite for success. In times of uncertainty, we must invest in growing human potential to stay fit for future purpose.

When we shift our focus to Level 4 leadership (people development), our attention is on the impact we have on people – more specifically, how we harness their potential. In this enhanced field of vision, we acknowledge that our primary responsibility as a leader is to produce leaders of the future (Maxwell, 2013). (We discuss the leadership skills required to meet future global challenges in Chapter 2.) Our role as change leaders requires us to step back to create an optimum environment for our high-potential team members to challenge themselves, learn new skills, grow their leadership capabilities, and take their organizations into the future.

Table 13.1 summarizes the key differences between the high-performance lawyer and the conscious lawyer. The high-performance lawyer delivers in the now. The conscious lawyer delivers for the future.

Table 13.1 Key differences between the high-performance lawyer and the conscious lawyer

High-performance lawyer	Conscious lawyer
Controls performance	Empowers everyone's strengths
Drives short-term results	Engages future thinking
Focuses on task completion	Inspires performance through learning
Motivates through ego	Humanizes a room

From profits to purpose

Traditionally, we have adopted a binary attitude to performance in the workplace, based on the assumption that profit and purpose are mutually exclusive – as though enjoying work means you are not trying hard enough to succeed. There is a new rhetoric at play that clearly states you can have both performance *and* fulfilment, with change on the side.

Mackey, McIntosh, and Phipps (2020, p. 4) strongly believe that we must put purpose first. Purpose helps everyone feel connected to their contributions, beyond financial success. It takes them to a place of higher meaning and impact, of making a difference in this world. Purpose also provides a context in which leaders can make decisions. When the answer is not clear-cut, clarity of purpose allows leaders to navigate through the grey in the direction of our 'true north' (Mackey, McIntosh, and Phipps, 2020, p. 6).

Conscious lawyers prioritize purpose over profits.

First, they deeply connect to their organizations' purpose – the vision, mission, and strategy. When we connect to our organizations' purpose with authenticity and meaning, and translate its relevance to what we do, we ignite the individual purpose that burns inside us. This means we behave in ways that embody the 'why' of our organizations. We speak the language of the organizations' purpose and communicate and role model this with our teams in all that we do.

Second, conscious lawyers take deliberate steps to show people how to implement their organizations' purpose on a day-to-day basis. When we uncover purpose at individual level, we work out the ambitions and motivations of our team members – what makes each of them 'tick'. Only when we help our team members to connect their individual purpose to the overall purpose of the organization will we unlock the pathway to fulfilling potential.

Conscious lawyers recognize their responsibility to connect to, and align themselves and their team members with, organizational purpose. When the conscious lawyer puts purpose first, the potential of the people around them becomes unlimited.

The state of being rather than doing

When we choose to lead consciously, we are choosing an infinite journey that teaches us a fundamental shift in attention from doing high performance to being a leader in our own lives. Our attention shifts from the destination to the process itself (as described in greater detail in Chapter 10).

Conscious lawyers focus their energies on being: first, an enabler; second, a facilitator; and, third, a coach.

Being an enabler

Conscious lawyers see their primary role in leadership as enabling others to fulfil their potential.

They are strategic in their thinking

Their primary focus becomes developing people, processes, procedures, and goals based on long-term, sustainable objectives to succeed. This means they ensure that information is relevant, transparently communicated and shared with the right people. They prioritize skills development in their team, particularly in areas of new learning critical to the future of their business. Knowledge and systems are demystified and training and learning emphasized.

They communicate vision

They express organizational vision in ways that resonate with each team member; they connect everyone's heart and mind to the vision to empower and engage them to achieve it. They take deliberate steps in explaining how the organizational vision translates into departmental vision, goals and objectives. They also explain to each team member how their efforts contribute to achieving these visions, goals and objectives to ensure each feels connected to their higher purpose.

They are future focused

Rather than being preoccupied by quarterly financial results and business targets, they are interested in creating long-term growth, profits, and purpose for the businesses they serve. They think about sustainable legacy and the impact they will have. They shift focus from pleasing their own boss and being the best, to caring about the organization's purpose, values and goals. They take steps to create strategy and plans as to how to get there. They are prepared to take a longer-term view of success; even at short-term cost to their financials.

They are courageous rather than strong

Using courage – strength from the heart – they take responsible decisions. They care about what is right and will not take decisions from a place of fear; to survive or be safe. They take decisions by connecting to their consciousness and tapping into the power of intuition, instinct, and experience.

They lead through change

They are not afraid to take risks and to step into the unknown and follow their beliefs. Rather than fear uncertainty, they embrace it; they make choices based on what they will learn. They understand what the optimum environment for creativity and innovation looks like and create this around their teams. They understand the risks that come from experimentation and make reasoned judgement calls, for which they hold themselves accountable.

And what difference does this make? It influences team members to change their mindset, direction, and behaviour. It can transform team performance from predictable to performance that achieves unprecedented gain. Table 13.2 summarizes what the conscious lawyer instils in team members and how this impacts them.

Table 13.2 What the conscious lawyer instils in team members and how this impacts them

What the conscious lawyer instils in team members	How this impacts team members
A shared vision of success	Feel part of a team brand
Accountability and responsibility	Understand the connection between organizational needs and individual talents and strengths
A culture of diversity and inclusion	Celebrate uniqueness within the team and the fact that everyone has a part to play
A collaborative growth culture	Feel part of an environment for experimentation, creativity, and innovation
A learning culture	See their success in terms of progress in thinking, learning, and stretching

Being a facilitator

Conscious lawyers understand their leadership essence to be creating the optimum environment for learning and growth.

They make connections

They get to know each of their team members, looking past subconscious biases, and uncover the strengths, weaknesses, and potential in all of them. They develop team members with stretch projects, challenges, and responsibilities. They encourage them to grow a network of their own stakeholder connections and take steps to sponsor and support them in doing so.

They prioritize communication

They focus on transparency, consistency, and contact. They believe there is no such thing as too much communication. They know there is no right answer, only choices in the moment. Well versed in having to deliver bad news sensitively, they have learnt that it is not what you say, but how you say it. Views are encouraged and respected, and thinking sessions are welcomed.

They create collaborative culture

Rather than encouraging a competitive environment focused on wins and being the best, they focus on the process of collaboration and the role of people in that. The emphasis is on growth through learning, ideas exchange, innovation, creativity, and stretching the envelope. They create a safe space where criticism, blame, and judgement are banished and mistakes are celebrated and learning emphasized.

They focus on potential

They organize roles, responsibilities, and tasks based on the unique talents and interests of each team member. Having uncovered team members' aspirations for growth and learning, they match goals and objectives that align with these. They connect their team members to how assigned tasks align with their goals and objectives, so achievement of potential becomes self-fulfilling.

They believe that everyone is capable and resourceful

They see their role as being to unleash capabilities in everyone. They believe in every individual's capacity to learn and grow with the right encouragement and support. If the environment is not right for the team member, they will treat them with respect and compassion in the journey of self-realization.

And what difference does this make? It connects business goals to each team member's capabilities in a meaningful way. Every team member connects to the organization's vision and strategy in a way that is unique and special to them, and this makes success self-fulfilling. In doing so, the conscious lawyer optimizes the realization of highest potential in the overall team.

Being a coach

Conscious lawyers hold space for the people around them to grow, learn, and contribute at their highest level.

They are emotionally intelligent

They have high levels of self-awareness and self-management. They have developed an ability to notice, and control, their emotions so that they can handle relationships with empathy and tact and achieve progress in a self-motivated way. They manage relationships with agility and are flexible in how they interact with people around them. They continue to build on their skills by actively seeking feedback from their team members and colleagues on their behaviour and performance.

They are values based

They have a firm understanding of the principles and beliefs that are at the core of who they are, and they behave in ways that honour those core values. When they make a choice, it is aligned with their values. They encourage their team members to be values based too, and show them how to do this. (For further details on values alignment, refer to Chapter 6.)

They trust

They believe in themselves and, therefore, trust themselves to be responsible and to use sound judgement. This belief and trust comes from their conscious-selves and is felt from the inside out. This gives their team members permission to believe in themselves too. And so trust is built.

They use coaching skills

They act as coach to their team members. They ask, listen, encourage, praise, recognize, and support. They shift their behaviour in specific ways:

- *Rather than command, they collaborate* – they create space for team members to perform actions according to how they choose to do them, not how leaders want them to do them.
- *Rather than control, they influence* – they treat others in ways that make them feel engaged and empowered.
- *Rather than tell, they ask* – they use open questions to help team members develop their own thinking on what, where, when, and how.
- *Rather than demand, they listen* – they hold space for team members when they need to be heard, and they actively seek their input, ideas, and contributions.
- *Rather than criticize, they encourage* – they prefer team members to practise leadership and see their primary role as supporting team members' development.

They measure their success not by results but by impact

They see success as progress. Rather than praise results, they recognize contributions, efforts, improvement, and growth as they occur. This focuses attention on the experience of learning and growth, which itself becomes satisfying and self-fulfilling.

And what difference does this make? It allows team members to be empowered to lead themselves, and it lets the leader focus on addressing difficulties and challenges as they arise. Rather than avoid or deflect problems or conflict, the conscious lawyer confronts challenge and actively seeks to resolve issues and differences to ensure obstacles are overcome.

Table 13.3 shows how a team member feels when they are led by a conscious lawyer.

Table 13.3 How a team member feels when they are led by a conscious lawyer

Engaged	I know what is expected of me and I am motivated to achieve these goals.
Included	I understand how my contribution impacts the bigger picture.
Connected	I feel part of something far greater than me.
Trusted	I know I can count on my colleagues.
Empowered	I feel I can accomplish anything I put my mind to.

With increasing pressure from technological disruption, rising global challenges, and generational shifts in the workplace, leaders have no option but to change the way they lead. Conscious lawyers shift their focus from producing high performance results to leading people. They put purpose first. By consciously choosing to stay in a state of being, conscious lawyers are versatile, agile, and open in the face of whatever is happening in the present moment of now. This ensures their focus remains on supporting people to lead themselves through the process of learning and growth. When lawyers choose to lead consciously, the potential of their team members becomes limitless.

Chapter 14
Transforming your impact

When we shift our attention from doing high performance to being a conscious lawyer, we focus on the impact we have on the people around us. Our attention shifts from achieving results to the process of change itself. When we take deliberate steps to create an optimum environment for learning and growth, the people around us proceed in flow. They feel challenged and fulfilled in equal measure. And change happens.

Motivating the new generation

Let's go back, for a moment, to the story in Chapter 1 of SP, the partner who, on the strength of the team feedback she received at her performance review, was assigned coaching in lieu of equity partnership. Her command-and-control leadership style was the outcome of accumulated pressure and stress of meeting high financial targets. But the dehumanizing impact it had on her team was also a function of who they were. Many of her team members were Millennials and Generation Z.

As discussed in Chapter 2, it is widely held that the new generation of lawyers in the workplace have different expectations and motivations to those who lead them. They may demand access to the opportunities they feel are right for them, crave activities that make them shine, and need complete autonomy and space to feel at their best. Espinoza, Ukleja, and Rusch (2010) note that working with this new generation requires an adaptive style rather than one that tries to coerce employees to change. Only by connecting team members to the higher purpose of their endeavours will they commit to the process of performing what is required of them.

This means that we need to change not only the way we work with this new generation of lawyers, but also the way we motivate them.

Transforming how we motivate takes versatility and some deliberate efforts to behave differently. Drawing from Espinoza, Ukleja, and Rusch (2010) plus my own experience of leading younger team members, there are a few tips to bear in mind.

They are purpose driven, so put meaning into their work

There is a tendency among the new generation of lawyers to need to feel connected to something greater; they want to make a difference in this world. As leaders, we must enable this. We must find opportunities that allow our teams to find greater meaning in their work. As soon as they understand the connection between their tasks or activities and the overarching vision or strategy, they are happy to comply (communicating vision is discussed in Chapter 13).

They work to live rather than live to work, so allow them flexibility

Being flexible means being open to team members' approaches to working and where they work. This is about returning autonomy back to them. Whilst they do not call all the shots, we must show willingness to be flexible about the ways they can meet their responsibilities and obligations.

They can get bored easily, so cultivate their imaginations

If team members are uninspired, demotivated, or feel like they are stagnating, they will simply quit. This means we need to find ways to trigger their imagination, self-expression, and blue-sky thinking. They will be most fulfilled when they are creating, innovating, or problem-solving.

They are 'children of praise', so praise them

It may be that some new-generation lawyers have grown up with constant attention, validation, and affirmation. But this does not mean they need us to anticipate all their needs and wants and respond accordingly. Rather, we should treat them with respect and find common ground.

They are not used to criticism, so encourage them

The new generation may have grown up being rescued by conservative, overprotective parents, so they may not respond well to negative feedback. This means we must show them how they can respond better to setbacks and take responsibility for learning from experience. To achieve this, we must banish judgement and blame and show them how to find learning by looking for the positives in difficult circumstances.

They can lack focus, so help them seek clarity

Whilst they may consider themselves to be great at multitasking, their approach may be viewed by some senior lawyers as disorganized. This means that to empower them to assume responsibility, we must be clear and specific in our instructions about our expectations.

In my own experience of leading younger team members, my skills as an executive coach have been fully exploited. Rather than tell, I ask. Rather than demand, I hold a space for group thinking and collaborate to agree what, when, and how. The most difficult aspect for me in adapting has been management of expectations. In the traditional, results-focused environment of legal teams, I simply delivered, regardless of fairness. I would pull an all-nighter rather than face the shame of missing an unreasonable deadline. This is simply not the case for many of the new generation of lawyers. In the absence of mutual respect, all bets are off. I learnt, from experience, to develop clear and agreed boundaries to ensure that when a late deadline descends, the young ones have not already left the building.

Our ability to lead the new generation of lawyers is dependent on our ability to continue to attract, retain, motivate, and develop them. For some leaders, this means that their focus must shift from treating the new generation the way they were treated earlier on in their careers. Instead, we must make their experience challenging, meaningful, and self-fulfilling.

Transforming the experience

When I look back at those times when I was primarily results focused, I recall high levels of effort, resistance, and conflict. I felt I needed to continually step in to check, measure, and course correct; pushing my team to achieve more, one task at a time. When I shifted focus from results to the process of flow – the experience of now – I started to relate to the people around me differently. I started to focus on what they needed and wanted in the moment, and my performance became seamless, fluid, and almost effortless.

As discussed in Chapter 11, it is the flow experience itself that drives individuals to creativity and outstanding achievement. It is the combination of sufficient challenge, which motivates us to perform, and focused attention, which draws us into the importance of now to such a degree the task becomes self-fulfilling. The limiting boundary of the conscious mind dissolves and in its place progress and learning emerge. When we complete a flow activity, our sense of self emerges larger than before due to the satisfaction and fulfilment we have gained (Csikszentmihalyi, 2008).

The key to enabling our teams to achieve greater fulfilment in what they do is to recreate their work as flow activities. These flow activities have unified goals that provide constant purpose. This means tasks, deals, and projects shift from being transactional in nature to transformative in themselves.

Transforming your team's work into an optimal experience of growth and learning requires moving from tasks to flow activities and from focusing on outcome to focusing on process (see Csikszentmihalyi, 2008, p. 157).

From tasks to flow activities

Traditional, results-focused lawyers are largely task orientated. Team members are designated specific roles in which they carry out certain types of work activities to achieve stated outcomes. When our focus shifts to performance as learning, we change the rhetoric from targets, results, and winning to focusing on progress, knowledge creation, and growth. The following sets out how this can be done.

Set meaningful goals that connect people to purpose

The term 'annual objectives' sends shivers down the spine of most partners and senior in-house lawyers. Setting objectives is commonly viewed as a tedious, bureaucratic administrative hurdle that sucks up hours that otherwise could be productive. This is because we have traditionally focused on making goals SMART – specific, measurable, attainable, realistic, and time-bound. But in this there is much lost opportunity. We can take the annual objectives exercise and transform it into inspiring and motivating our teams to find greater meaning in life and work.

Your team members want to know the purpose of their role, its impact on achieving vision and strategy, and how specific contributions will lead to fulfilment of purpose. Objectives can shift from a static 'to-do list' to a dynamic dashboard that sets out meaningful goals connected to strategy and purpose, tracks progress, and provides recognition and feedback on achievement of certain milestones. The team member has greater autonomy and feels more in control of the process of goal achievement. As a natural consequence, they are willing to accept more responsibility and exercise greater initiative and creativity in achieving goals. Things to note, in particular:

- It is all about the 'why'. You need to be clear on how the goals connect to the overriding team or departmental strategy ('How does this connect to the bigger picture?').
- You need to be clear on how the goals connect the team member to their motivations and purpose ('What's in it for me?').
- Focus cannot be purely on performance related to short-term goals such as targets, financial results, bonuses. You need to include learning goals that go to core competencies, changes in capabilities, and sustainable, long-term development. These are goals like 'increase understanding of changes in...', 'overcome fear of...', and 'enhance skills in....'.

For an exercise in setting strategy, goals, and objectives, visit www.kiranscarr.com/downloads.

Make work activities complex and challenging

According to Csikszentmihalyi, challenges create potential for complexity, and complexity creates scope for enjoyment and fulfilment (2008, p. 149). As discussed in Chapter 2, the new generation of lawyers may not draw a distinct line between work and play so are attracted to tasks and activities that permit them to have fun. By gamifying the process, you provide your team members the opportunity to connect to joy and fulfilment.

When you gamify the process, team members are given high-level parameters, such as the 'what' and the 'why', and are left to choose how they get there. They are given scope to work out the problem themselves. You should encourage them to seek help and guidance when needed, but otherwise leave it to them. Trust them, in the knowledge that mistakes are not wrong – they are learning. The more a job inherently resembles a game – variety, appropriate and flexible challenges, clear goals, and immediate feedback – the more enjoyable it will be. Rather than impose boundaries and structure, give them opportunities for expressing their freedom and creativity (see Csikszentmihalyi, 2008, p. 152).

What I observe most when I draw a team member into flow activity is that by me stepping out, unlimited space is created in which their wisdom, creativity, innovation, and learning thrives.

From focusing on outcome to focusing on process

When we made the transformation from being results orientated at Level 3 leadership (production) to being impact orientated at Level 4 leadership (people development) (Maxwell, 2013), we learnt how to shift our focus from the destination to the process of change itself (refer to Chapter 10 for details of choosing greater impact). Similarly, as conscious lawyers, when we shift our focus to creating an optimum environment for high performance, we start to train team members to recognize the benefits and gains of the process itself over the results or outcomes achieved. We have already done the work in the background of connecting their activities to the bigger picture of purpose and value. We now bring their attention and focus to the opportunities for action, developing skills, and reaching goals through their efforts. In doing so, our team members start to see the impact in the now and derive immediate satisfaction from that.

Based on Csikszentmihalyi's (2008) recommendations and my experience of leading teams through legal and compliance transformation projects, I have learnt that there are a few tricks to adopt with team members to help them appreciate process over outcome.

Mentor towards making conscious choices

Workplaces often encourage automatic or default responses and choices (Csikszentmihalyi, 2008, p. 210). Consciously mentor your team members to silence default and, instead, dial up their existing skills and engage in stretching or developing those skills. This is of particular importance for younger team members who may not receive criticism well and look to be rescued when things go wrong. Encourage them to be curious and challenge assumptions about themselves and their abilities. When a team member pays attention to developing a specific skill, they pay attention to what they learn from each action. When they start to see a pattern of consistency, they enjoy a sense of progress and development unfolds. As this is self-rewarding, it leads to motivation to do more of the same to gain better results, and the entire process becomes self-fulfilling.

Learn to enjoy immediate experience

Being in control of what you are consciously choosing to do means that anything that happens can be a source of enjoyment (Csikszentmihalyi, 2008, p. 213). There is much to experience in the conscious act of learning – noticing small details, seeing the beauty in simple things, receiving immediate feedback on trying something different and seeing where it takes you. Giving team members the opportunity to do something in the interests of learning ignites their passion for learning something new. Encourage departures into learning, name experiments for what they are, and encourage your team to find more opportunities to experience the feeling of enjoyment through learning.

Become immersed in the activity

Be open to environments that allow for immersion in activity (Csikszentmihalyi, 2008, p. 210) in bouts of creativity and productivity. With the Covid-19 pandemic, even the most traditional lawyers no longer mistake presenteeism for performance. With the new generation, flexibility is key. Allow them to occupy environments that encourage creativity and give them flexibility to choose when they contribute. Encourage breaks and prioritize activities that nourish productivity, like eating away from their desks and moving around during the day. It is possible to receive higher output with less input.

Pay attention to what is happening

Stepping out to create space for your team does not mean being blinkered to what is occurring. You must focus on what is happening over time to ensure your team members remain on track, particularly those who struggle to retain focus. Their role is to keep concentration through constant 'inputs of attention' (Csikszentmihalyi, 2008, p. 211). Your role is to sustain their involvement at a distance, allowing space for team members to course correct and learn as part of their process. This creates responsibility for both parties to keep connected to what is happening and seek feedback, reassurance, and input. But take care not to sever team members' connection to responsibility for leading themselves through the process of learning.

Have coaching conversations

The move in learning organizations away from annual performance reviews to continual review procedures is for a valid reason: the need to embrace performance as learning. Shift your focus from achieving results to performance as learning so that performance appraisals stop being about improving employees' strengths and weaknesses and become more of a continued dialogue about what your team members are experiencing and what this means for their future growth and learning. Have regular meetings with team members where the primary focus is on where they are in their development and what challenges they are facing. Sometimes they just need to vent. If so, hold a space for their thinking out loud, to enable them to take greater responsibility for their journey of learning. Sometimes, they need emotional support and encouragement or mentoring. If so, help them make more conscious choices.

Table 14.1 shows what the optimum experience of learning feels like for team members.

Table 14.1 The optimum experience of learning from the perspective of a team member

In the optimum environment for learning:
<ul><li>Vision and strategy is connected to my capabilities and activities in a meaningful way.</li><li>My mindset shift focuses me on deriving enjoyment from the process itself.</li><li>I feel supported, listened to, encouraged, and empowered.</li><li>I am encouraged to experiment and I celebrate opportunities for learning.</li></ul>

When we focus on process over outcome, we believe in the process itself. Whilst we still have our Excel spreadsheet for results and targets open on our desktop, we are not looking at this as our primary proof of performance. We are observing and watching our team members – their behaviours, interactions, and moods – as indicators of the activities of challenge, stretching, trying, and asking for support.

If team members are behaving in ways that demonstrate they are focused on the process of performance as learning, we are consciously leading them through change. By transforming their experience of performance as learning, we are tapping into their unlimited capacity to convert potential into achievement through their own efforts (refer to Figure 9.1).

When we create the optimum environment for learning, the people around us empower themselves to grow.

Leaders of law firms and corporate legal departments are facing unprecedented challenges that require them to change the way they lead from delivering results to having greater impact. They must lead people through change, which requires a shift to creating an optimum environment for the people around them to learn and grow. By courageously transforming people's experience of performance as learning, we unleash their unlimited potential. In doing so, we create change leaders of the future.

LEAP III in a nutshell

- When we fail to lead ourselves, we leave a negative imprint on the people around us that can have lasting impact. We make them feel demotivated and dehumanized, leading to a downward spiral in performance. The cost of this damage is high.
- With increasing pressure from technological disruption, rising global challenges, and generational shifts in the workplace, the lawyer who is leading through change must harness greater potential in people. They must motivate their teams to collaborate and innovate to radically change how legal services are delivered.
- Leading people through change means focusing on our sphere of influence to deepen our relationships with those who can best contribute to our value through partnership, collaboration, and mutual support.
- When we lead people through change, we shift from high performance results that focus on what we achieve to conscious leadership that focuses on how we all learn.
- Conscious lawyers are values based and take deliberate action to elevate their leadership from Level 3 (production) to Level 4 (people development) (Maxwell, 2013). They put purpose first, which means they prioritize long-term, sustainable rewards over short-term profits.

- Conscious lawyers shift attention from doing leadership to being leaders in their own lives, which means they:
  - see their primary role in leadership as enabling others to fulfil their potential;
  - understand their leadership essence as facilitating the creation of an optimum environment for learning and growth; and
  - hold space for their team members to operate at their highest level of contribution by coaching them to learn and grow.
- With growth mindset, our attention shifts to the process of change itself. We change *the experience of work* into something that is challenging, meaningful, and self-fulfilling. We recreate work as flow activities by applying two strategies:
  - from tasks to flow – we set meaningful goals that connect to purpose and make work activities complex and challenging
  - from focusing on outcome to focusing on process – through mentoring, coaching, and support, we help people appreciate process over outcome.
- By transforming people's experience of performance as learning, we consciously lead them through the process of using their efforts to convert unlimited potential to achievement.

LEAP IV:

Entrust others to fulfil their potential

We look for power outside ourselves.

We look to who we can control
And what we can demand.

Ignoring that mightiness comes not from
controlling others
But from surrendering to them.

Letting go gives freedom.

Letting go gives space.

Letting go gives opportunity.

The source of our deepest power
Comes from trusting others.

When we believe in ourselves,
We trust others

And their success makes us rise.

Chapter 15
Why trust matters

In Leap III, we learn that to lead through change, we must focus, every day, on maintaining an optimum environment for growth – one of engagement, empowerment, inclusion, collaboration, and trust. In Leap IV, we deepen our understanding of what builds trust and inclusion in the workplace. We look deeper at how we must transfer ownership of potential back into the hands of the people around us so that they can be leaders of the future of law.

Fixed mindset erodes trust

We explore in Chapter 9 how sitting in fixed mindset limits us. The belief that our personal traits are fixed creates urgency to constantly be proving ourselves. Each situation calls for an opportunity to reaffirm our intelligence, wit, or dominance. We actively seek opportunities that confirm we are superior to the others in the room. We avoid change, in fear of any opportunity that may cause us to fail. The fixed mindset sufferer has one primary motivation: self-validation.

Much of this pursuit of validation is born out of recruitment policies, since the 1990s, of major organizations bent on attracting and recruiting the 'best talent'. The assumption underpinning this approach was that graduates from the best universities, groomed for success, would be the natural leaders of the future because of their 'innate' talent and ability, which separates them from the crowd. Once recruited, they would be 'fast-tracked' through the system – attracting priority in sponsorship, mentorship, and development – to ensure that when the opportunity arose for advancement, they were ready to accede. I certainly recall the difference in access to opportunity granted to white, male, Oxbridge graduates in a 'magic circle' law firm. The rest of us had to prove our worthiness at every turn while observing the 'anointed souls' overtake us on the travelator to the partnership lounge.

In an environment that promotes on preconceptions of innate talent, image becomes the primary marker of success. This means we are uncomfortable with circumstances that jeopardize the images we seek to uphold. This shows up most dramatically in the person with fixed mindset having difficulty admitting their mistakes. When something goes wrong, they fear being exposed. Their preoccupation with image creates an inner monologue focused on judging and criticizing themselves. They look for mechanisms outside themselves to validate that they are smart, successful, and talented. They use people around them to service their egos and insulate them from failure. Some fall guys are blamed; others are sacrificed. (We discuss when ego stops serving us in greater detail in Chapter 4.)

And the ultimate impact of this on the ability of fixed mindset leaders to lead others? Trust is eroded. People may listen to them, but they do so because they have to, not because they want to. People may show the leader respect, but that does not mean they respect who the leader really is. They may behave in a way that suggests they have faith in the leader's ability to judge and capacity to act, but that does not mean they feel trust in their hearts.

The problem we face when we are stuck in fixed mindset is that the people around us simply do not trust us.

Without trust, there is no leadership

Returning to the story in Chapter 12 of MH, the coaching client who felt disempowered and demotivated at the hands of a high-performing general counsel. MH respected her general counsel tremendously for her technical expertise and ability to lead a room. However, notwithstanding these qualities, MH resented the general counsel's authoritative leadership approach and fixed mindset ways, which made MH feel blocked and controlled. Regardless of the general counsel's capabilities and experience, MH feared that if something went wrong, the general counsel would simply not have her back.

In their recent study of 87,000 leaders, Zenger and Folkman (2019) examined the foundations of trust in the context of corporate leadership and discovered that level of trust is highly correlated with how people rate the leader's overall leadership effectiveness. Of the three core elements of trust identified – positive relationships, judgement, and consistency – it was positive relationships that had the most substantial impact on trust. When judgement and consistency were high but positive relationships low, the trust rating diminished disproportionately. Zenger and Folman conclude that if positive relationships are never built or become damaged, it is difficult for people to trust in leadership.

So, trust is critical to our effectiveness as leaders. Regardless of how competent we are technically or how well we manage processes, we are not behaving as leaders if we do not build relationships with the people around us. Managers lead processes and results. Leaders lead people.

When we believe in the people around us, they feel our belief. When people trust the belief we have in them, they connect to the belief they have in themselves. When we create this circle of trust, we are connecting everyone to their ability to fulfil their highest potential. The result is they feel empowered to do whatever it takes to make their highest contribution.

Without trust, tasks will simply be completed with predictable results, based on the level of effort made. In an empowered culture of trust, outcomes are enriching, incalculable, and often exponential.

What builds trust in the workplace

Think back to a line manager who you deeply and implicitly trusted. What was it about this line manager that engendered this trust? How and what did they communicate? How did you know who and what they cared about? How did they make you feel when you were unsure or under pressure?

Botsman (2018) explains how technology is changing the way we trust ourselves and others. She notes that there has been extensive review and commentary of the core traits of trustworthiness, with many researchers, authorities, and thought leaders proposing their own version of the core components of trust. Botsman concludes that three characteristics commonly recur: competence, integrity, and reliability (Botsman, 2018, p. 292).

When we venture deeper into the concept of trust in the workplace, we discover that trust does not exist by itself, but as a growing organism that feeds off the environment within which it lives. Reina and Reina (1999) believe in the transactional nature of trust, explaining that it is reciprocal (you must give it to receive it) and created incrementally. They outline three types of transactional trust: trust of capability, trust of character, and trust of communication (Reina and Reina, 1999).

I like to think of trust in terms of growing a 'trust tree', as represented in Figure 15.1.

Figure 15.1 The core components of growing a trust tree

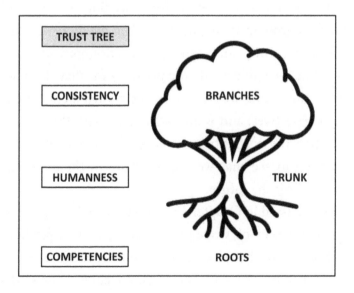

There are three core components of the trust tree:

- *The roots* – these ground us in the bedrock of trust: respect, faith, belief. These are our 'competencies', and these need to be continually nourished and fed.
- *The trunk* – this continually boosts and supports the building of trust between us and the people around us. This is our 'humanness', so often underestimated and underutilized.
- *The branches* – these stretch and grow at will. This is our 'consistency' (our constant attention to our purpose of connecting others to their potential).

Tending to the roots

Our skills and ability enabled us to reach leadership positions. Trust in us was largely built on the foundation of people respecting our capabilities and believing that they can depend on us and learn from us. But as the people around us grow in their potential, they need greater challenge, opportunity for growth, and autonomy, and they expect that we will provide the platform for that. They will look for signs that we believe in their judgement, require their perspectives, and want partnership with them that is more than the conventional teacher–student relationship. They need to see that we are investing in them to build something for the future.

As discussed in Chapter 13, conscious leadership is built on a foundation of strategic, visionary, and inspirational direction. As we become more senior, dependence on our process-driven traits – our specialisms, technical knowledge, and skills – will decrease our credibility rather than enhance it. The less we change, the more trust is eroded. If our involvement or impact sets others back, we become obstacles to their progress and achievement.

This means we simply need to do the work. People will only trust us when we trust ourselves. This comes from stepping into growth mindset to better know our competencies, our blind spots, and what lies beneath and unhealed (we deal with connecting to greater consciousness in Chapter 7 and moving into growth mindset in Chapter 9). Only when we know ourselves and hold this in esteem can we start to trust ourselves and apply it in building deeper, more sustainable trust with others.

Being the trunk

Honesty, openness, integrity. These are the core values that many lawyers ascribe to their sense of self. But it is not enough to go through the motions of *doing* what is expected of us when we are upholding these values (we discuss this in Chapter 6). We also must *feel* these actions. We must act on them in a way that is human. When we have built a reputation based on certain qualities, people expect us to behave in ways that are consistent with those qualities. This takes emotional intelligence, particularly the ability to manage our emotions to have positive impact on others around us.

To ensure that trust thrives in the environment in which we lead, we are responsible for showing empathy and compassion.

Our ability to empathize

Words are not enough. We need to behave in a way that shows others that what we say is what we mean. We need to be able to step to the side of the other person and see things from their perspective. Sympathy involves understanding the plight of others from our own perspectives. We ask ourselves what we would feel in their shoes. Empathy, on the other hand, involves listening to how the person feels and putting ourselves in their shoes to try and understand *why* they may have these feelings. In becoming aware of the underlying reasons for why a person feels the way they do, we are in a more informed position to support their recovery and growth.

Our ability to apply compassion

Actions are not enough. We may be motivated to help, but we need to want to help in our hearts. Compassion is the feeling that arises when we are confronted with another's discomfort or suffering and feel motivated to take positive steps to relieve that ill ease. We feel compelled to act on our feelings of concern for the person. We move beyond empathy and show that we are willing to act for their sake.

Let us take the example of delegating a matter to a team member. We could exclaim 'You can do this!', but we must mean it too. We must invoke empathy, which means we must step to their side and see the task through their eyes in the knowledge of their strengths and limiting beliefs. We must connect to the memory of how it feels to be in a state of discomfort due to not knowing whether we can do it. In that moment, we need to open our hearts to have compassion for the team member (we discuss finding compassion in Chapter 7). When we open our hearts in this way, the team member can feel the belief and trust we have in them. And feeling that trust gives them permission to trust themselves. Trust that they can achieve whatever they put their minds to. Trust that they can do it.

Often, we speak the words 'You can do this!' from our ego-selves rather than from our conscious-selves (we discuss this in Chapter 7). Our lips say the words, but our hearts do not mean it. Our hearts are closed because we are in protective mode, in fear of failure and thinking to ourselves: 'We are on a deadline, and we just need to get this done!' Maybe we are too busy or too stretched or too tired or too complacent to really care how the other person feels. Maybe we just want this problem off our desk. And the implications of this are that the task gets done but the imprint has been made – the trust is not felt. The opportunity cost of the absence of trust is undeveloped potential, undelivered excellence, and absence of creativity and innovation.

If we want people around us to fulfil their highest potential, we need to humanize ourselves (not dehumanize them). We need to empathize with them and take steps to show them how much we care about them and how they feel.

Encouraging the branches

It is the role of the team member to seek out and use the available resources around them to reach and grow to their highest potential. It is the role of the leader to ensure that there is a constant source of sustenance for the team member's growth. This may mean intervening to overcome hurdles or resolve conflicts. It may mean facilitating their learning, challenging their assumptions, or giving them a bit of a leg up when needed. But in truth, it is about being a consistent role model and mentor. Being reliable by being there, honouring commitments, and keeping promises. It is simply being in a way that they know they can depend on you.

To enable trust to continue to grow, focus is diverted from who we are to how we impact others. We pay constant attention to our purpose of enabling the realization of potential in others (how conscious lawyers enable potential is discussed in Chapter 13). This means reducing disruption to their growth by eliminating white noise and other distractions, ensuring consistent availability of resources and support, and providing regular positive feedback and communication to enable improvement and learning.

Building trust in the workplace takes constant attention to caring about growth of ourselves and the people around us.

How growth mindset allows trust

We explore in Chapter 9 how growth mindset is based on the belief that our qualities can be cultivated through efforts. We also explore in Chapter 11 how people experience learning through flow activities that fulfil and challenge them in equal measure.

When we commit our efforts to embracing challenges and receive feedback in the form of learning, we become more open to trust. We experience what it is like to feel motivated through improvement and growth. We become more at ease in tackling setbacks and find inspiration in our mistakes and errors. We start to role model this resilience to the people around us. They start to see that persistent effort is a path to mastery and are emboldened to try it too.

When we go on the journey of shifting to growth mindset, we see how it builds trust, first in ourselves and then with those around us.

Building trust in ourselves

When we adopt a mindset of wanting to develop our own abilities, we start to believe in ourselves. We start to believe in our capability to be better, to fulfil even higher potential. We tend to our roots, which means we take action to know ourselves better and uncover what is harming us. We take on the issues we discover to be holding us back – our critical inner dialogue, limiting assumptions, and unhealed wounds from the past (we discuss freeing ourselves from limiting beliefs in Chapter 9). Quite simply, we nurture ourselves.

In adopting growth mindset, we change our inner monologue from one of criticism, judgement, or resentment to one of improvement and growth. We start to learn that compassion for others starts first with compassion for ourselves (we discuss finding compassion in Chapter 7). Instead of submerging or denying the darker aspects of ourselves, we see these as scars in need of attention. We see the beauty in the lessons they give us, show gratitude for those lessons, and start to tend to the scars with love (we discuss tending to blind spots and scars in Chapter 7). Rather than being stiff and unyielding, we become flexible to whatever we need to accommodate and support.

We learn to trust who we are. By applying respect, belief, and compassion towards ourselves, we become more open and able to show trust in others.

Building trust in others

Attending to our own self-beliefs frees us to encourage others to do the same. Having to deal with the shift from fixed mindset to growth mindset makes us more attuned to the process of learning and growth. We know how it feels to be motivated by a process of change and flow. We recall in our hearts how it felt to feel fulfilled by the process of learning itself.

In our own experience of growth, we learnt to trust that potential converts to achievement through effort (refer to Chapter 9). Our role as growth leaders is to connect others to their own limitless ability to do this too. When we connect to our light, we want to show others how to shine their light too. But we cannot turn the light on for others; that is their journey to take. They must go on the journey themselves to learn how to trust, first themselves and then others. Because the learning lies in the journey itself.

When we believe in ourselves, we trust in our ability to learn. This means that even if we do not know whether we can trust someone, we go ahead and trust them anyway. We trust them and detach from the outcome of that trust. Because when we place trust in the hands of the people around us, we put trust in them learning for themselves.

Courageous leaders of growth learn whether they can trust people by simply putting trust in them.

Chapter 16

Making learning your success criteria

When we adopt growth mindset and accept that performance is learning, our focus is squarely on how we improve the process of learning. Our role as leaders of change is to role model the implicit benefits of change to the people around us. When we connect others to their limitless capacity for growth, we harness the true power of potential in people.

Why inclusion matters

I cannot think of anything more destructive to the human soul than feeling excluded. Having connection to, and caring about, something far greater than ourselves is what makes us human. We are inherently social and rely on cooperation to survive and thrive. When we feel our endeavours are siloed from the activities of others, we start to question our positions, motivations, and efforts. Everyone experiences divisive treatment in the workplace in some form in their career. It may have been a microaggression caused by subconscious bias or exclusion from a meeting due to the dictates of hierarchy. The impact is the same: we feel unworthy.

Inclusion is wide and broad in its impact. It can be institutional, such as being part of a discussion or decision-making process, or it can be embedded in a personal leadership style, such as collaborative thinking. It can relate to how we are treated in our roles or simply to whether we are seen for who we are. Inclusion creates trust, belonging, fulfilment, and connection, and it can lead to greater engagement and productivity. For instance, research found that a 10% increase in perceptions of inclusion reduced absenteeism, adding almost one day a year of attendance per employee (Deloitte Australia and Victorian Equal Opportunity and Human Rights Commission, 2013).

At a fundamental level, we want to be included because we see the correlation this has to financial reward. But it goes much further than this. People care about organizational culture. They see that healthy relationships in the workplace create more opportunity to learn, improve skills, and fulfil potential. Learning and enjoyment are inherent aspects of work. Without these elements, we stagnate or, worse still, we diminish, become less of ourselves. And that is why we are evolving our workplaces to learning organizations. Senge (2006) describes a learning organization as a place where people continually expand their capacity to achieve what they truly desire and develop new patterns of thinking to see the whole reality of what they create. When an organization brings us together to feel connection to a bigger vision of ourselves, we feel united in a belief in our own capacity to grow and achieve a higher purpose. And it is this connection to purpose that gives our performance greater meaning and motivates us to go above and beyond to reach our highest potential. (We discuss communicating vision and shifting from profits to purpose in Chapter 13.)

Inclusion also leads to greater knowledge equity in organizations. By fostering an inclusive culture, the rhetoric changes from being about individual contributions to being about collaborative learning. For example, when people are encouraged in a meeting to contribute to each other's thinking, ideas creation, and decision-making, the potential of the overall room increases. Attention shifts from individual performance as an outcome to collaborative performance as learning. When we accept that performing and learning are one and the same, we focus on finding ways to optimize collaboration in the workplace. This means focusing on ways to better convert potential into achievement through collaborative efforts.

By valuing people's collaborative contribution, we harness the power of collective wisdom.

Harnessing collective wisdom

Growth leaders subscribe to a lifetime of learning. They appreciate their own shortcomings and the limits of their own expertise. They know they are not a specialist in everything and are willing to solicit expertise from the people around them. They role model responsible decision-making by seeking input or consensus when required. Quite simply, they harness the power of collective wisdom.

Based on my experience of working with other growth leaders in leading through change, the hallmarks of harnessing collective wisdom are:

- *Attacking elitism* – disband unnecessary committees and venture outside the hierarchical senior leadership structure to seek specific input and expertise.
- *Surrounding ourselves well* – have the right people in the room, regardless of convention and position.
- *Being open to new ideas* – welcome change initiatives and new ideas regardless of source.
- *Hiring the right people* – select people for their passion and mindset, not their pedigree and political savvy.
- *Rewarding the right behaviours* – apply performance metrics that reward collaboration and innovation, not just results.
- *Prioritizing diversity and inclusion* – believe in the collective wisdom of diverse viewpoints and actively seek opportunities to integrate diversity of thought in meetings, committees, and decision-making panels.
- *Being customer-centric* – look beyond results to focus on feedback from end users on execution and experience.

Learning organizations are putting in place formal structures to ensure that they capitalize on knowledge that exists at all levels. Shadow boards, for example, operate extremely well when communicating, designing, and implementing strategic change initiatives using the skills and perspectives of less senior personnel. Because many of the new generation of workforce feel entitled to opportunity and value rewards (we discuss this in greater detail in Chapter 2), giving them seats at the decision-making table creates incentives that bind them to realizing organizational purpose.

The role of a growth leader is to develop leaders of the future. We can use the collective wisdom of our future leaders in the now. But we must also look to the future of change. We must prepare the people around us for growth.

Making room for growth

In Chapter 9, we explored the benefits of shifting our leadership mindset to one of growth. With fresh experience of the process of learning for ourselves, we realize how much we learn from everyone and everything around us. Our team members are there to teach us as much as we are there to teach them. It is a symbiotic relationship that is self-fulfilling and ever evolving. Similarly, when we speak of mentorship, we often assume that one party is the mentor and the other the mentee. In truth, the beauty of a mentoring relationship is that both parties feed and nourish each other. When I hold a space for a client, I do so with curiosity, hoping they will trigger in me ideas, perspectives, and reflections that I have not encountered before. In the knowledge that I do not hold all the answers, I am keen to learn more about what is in their awareness and experience that can spark greater transformation in me.

The benefit of learning from others is that we are role modelling what growth mindset looks like back to them. Because growth mindset is in our heads and not directly visible to others, it is demonstrated by how we behave. When we say something or act in certain ways that show commitment to growth and learning, that is what others pick up on. And we give them permission to behave and act in similar ways. We pass growth mindset on.

KC is the newly promoted head of business development in a regional office of an international law firm. She was promoted to lead the whole-scale transformation of the firm's business development function after significant downsizing during the Covid-19 pandemic. KC came to me for mentorship to support her through the process of change. At our first session, she confided in me that she felt like a failure. Four months into the role, KC had successfully completed the challenging job of reorganizing roles, uplevelling job descriptions, and re-crafting objectives and goals to align with streamlined operations. She had also engaged the team in preparing revised policies and procedures to take account of changes in how the function would operate going forward. This was effective in creating transparency for her team members in relation to their roles and responsibilities. However, it did not seem to have had the positive change in behaviour she had expected. 'They keep coming to me with questions, looking to me to step in and solve problems for them. They don't resolve any issues themselves – they just argue with each other or question the changes we've made. I'm starting to doubt whether we can work effectively as a team.'

After exploring the team environment and dynamics in more detail, I concluded that KC had missed a critical first step in leading through change. Whilst she had created clarity on what, when, and how her people should perform, she had omitted to consider the inner workings of the people themselves.

KC had neglected the 'humanness' aspect of building trust in changing behaviour (we discuss building trust in Chapter

15). She bypassed transforming the experience for her team in favour of quick wins and demonstrating change (we discuss transforming the experience of work from tasks to meaningful and fulfilling activities in Chapter 14). It was not enough to be open-minded and flexible, encouraging her team members to try all these new approaches and procedures. Having endured a series of redundancies and a prolonged period of Covid-19 challenges, KC and her team were most likely in fixed mindset (we discuss the features of fixed mindset in Chapter 9). This meant that many viewed change with suspicion and feared disruption to the status quo. Whilst their bodies could move in the direction of change, their heads were saying no. Had KC, in the initial weeks after her promotion, focused on uncovering the motivations and expectations of her team members, she would probably have seen how heavily steeped the team was in fixed mindset and how much encouragement and recognition would have to be given before they would be willing and able to shift from fear to courage.

KC and I started the journey of cultivating her own ability and the ability of her team to move from fixed mindset to growth mindset.

Mentoring a shift to growth mindset

As KC proceeded with this change project, we worked quickly on shifting her to growth mindset (we discuss how to move from fixed mindset to growth mindset in Chapter 9). KC practised how to shift her focus from achieving high performance results to cultivating potential in the people around her (we discuss how to shift from doing leadership to being a leader in Chapter 10). Soon enough, KC started to transform the experience for her team through creation of the optimum environment for growth and learning (we discuss the process of transforming your impact in Chapter 14).

I mentored KC through the following key differences in approach, based on recommendations by Dwek (2017, p. 219), to better enable the transition through change.

Focusing on people's motivations towards change

As an initial step, we must appraise our team members, not only in terms of competence and performance but also, more fundamentally, in terms of who they are. We must notice and observe the detail of them, without judgement. We must make up our own minds about their capacity for change and willingness to learn. We often have strong instincts as to someone's motivation, but it is crucial to silence our brains from the white noise of preconceptions and assumptions, particularly the subjective opinions of others, to arrive at a true view of what we know. You may even have to assign growth mindset scores as part of your assessment of team members, largely to help you ascertain which people are more likely to become your champions in the change process. When we are leading through change, it is helpful to know who will learn fastest, who will slow change down a gear, and who may even be trying to sabotage progress based on their fears.

Praising the process of learning

Even if we have growth mindset, we may find we are pointing to the negatives of the past or focusing on ability in the present rather than turning attention to the overall learning process. We may have learnt how to praise effort rather than outcome, but leading transformational change requires us to praise the process that the people around us are engaged in (Dwek, 2017, p. 219).

For instance, the animated encouragement of 'You're doing a great job!' and 'Keep up the good work!' fall on deaf ears after prolonged use. In some cases, this starts to demotivate rather than accelerate change. When we praise parts of the process that lead to greater learning, people seem to connect and open up to further learning. Examples are praising the specific effort employed, the strategy used, or the type of resilience shown. When we tie that process to the goal – learning, progress, achievement – this forms deeper understanding of cause and effect. Deeper learning connections form. Growth mindset starts to embed within them.

Showing the learning from mistakes and past experiences

The way we respond to setbacks, mistakes, and failures will have the greatest impact on enabling people to shift to growth mindset. If we respond with anxiety or question capacity to recover, we can foster fixed mindset. As discussed in Chapter 9, when we are in fixed mindset and we fail, the act of failure becomes an identity. If we think of ourselves as failures, we will stop in our tracks and refuse to take any further steps to change, because we believe in our hearts that it is impossible for us to improve and are nonresponsive to feedback to the contrary. We get stuck and this impacts others and their ability to change too.

Instead, we can address problems head on. Communicate mistakes as setbacks (Dwek, 2017, p. 219). Corrections are a good thing that should be embraced and used as opportunity for learning. When an error or failure occurs, we can respond with interest and curiosity, and treat the event as a platform for exploration and further experiment. When we do this, we are behaving in a way that transmits growth mindset. Mistakes become something to openly discuss rather than deny, and people are drawn together in sharing the learning that flows.

Teaching for understanding not performance

As results-focused leaders, we often talk in terms of measuring performance by what is achieved, as if accomplishments are a series of static locksteps towards an ultimate state of success. When we accept that the goal is learning, our focus shifts to helping people acquire the skills to think for themselves and be resourceful so that they can make continuous progress through problems and challenges. When we step to the side of our team members in the experience of change, we see it from their perspectives. We see that they gain most from having conceptual understanding of what they do, what is expected of them, and how they should proceed. This means we must care about *understanding* what is being faced more than we care about the act of doing. Dwek comments that when we care about deeper understanding and work with our team to achieve this, the team members are more likely to believe their abilities can be developed (Dwek, 2017, p. 219).

During the change journey with KC, she acknowledged the early steps she had bypassed in the process of change and made a point to cover them off. Understanding the need to transform everyday tasks to flow activities, KC dedicated time to communicating vision and strategy to her team members and explaining how their objectives and goals connected each of them to the bigger picture (we discuss transforming experience in Chapter 14). She shifted her focus from delivering change to the process of change, prioritizing people-focused time, such as individual coaching support to team members (we discuss the role of leader as coach in Chapter 13).

By transforming her team's experience of change into one of understanding, KC dramatically shifted her own and her team's performance from doing change to being the change the organization needed.

Connecting at human level

The role of a growth leader in the process of change is to lead people through that change, being open and honest about what they see and experience. To build trust in the process, it is important to be connected to our vulnerabilities and show our humanness. This requires constant dialogue not only on the process itself but also on what is happening to us through the process. This means acknowledging the difficulties and challenges of growth and learning, and sharing strategies for how we can show greater compassion for ourselves and others during these times.

It is also about creating urgency in team members' minds so that they are motivated to change the behaviours that no longer serve them. Kotter (2012) identifies the first definitive step in leading change as creating urgency. This is a critical step, necessary to foster the right climate for change. Holding a safe space for your team members to share their concerns, fears, and insecurities comes with a responsibility to connect them to the realities of facing global challenges. As we lead them through change, we must raise awareness of the opportunity cost of not adopting a mindset of growth and learning in the context of their future careers and realizing their potential.

As growth leaders, when we start to trust ourselves, we start to show the people around us what trust in ourselves looks like. By showing our own willingness to learn and grow as change leaders, we are role modelling how it is to lead through change. In doing so, we connect our team members to their capacity to lead themselves through change. We are preparing the people around us to be change leaders of the future.

Chapter 17

Creating change leaders of the future

As growth leaders of change, we role model to the people around us what it is to be a change leader of the future. But we are, above all, conscious lawyers. We see our success not in who chooses to follow us, but in how those people choose to lead. We empower the people around us to succeed beyond our expectations.

Whose potential do we own?

CP is a former colleague who struggled with his fixed mindset. After he moved into a new in-house role in a start-up technology service provider, he came to me for coaching support, as he knew he needed assistance with breaking through an impasse. In the eight months since his move, his legal team's overall performance had deteriorated. At first the team were cohesive, ambitious, and responsive. In the fast-paced environment of an entrepreneurial enterprise, what the team lacked in attention to detail and accuracy (done is better than perfect) they very much made up for in proactivity and creativity. But CP was a true perfectionist, intolerant of any delay or mistake (we discuss pursuit of perfection in Chapters 7 and 9). If a team member showed any signs of error, missed a deadline, or gave unclear advice, he would swoop in to fix the problem. He would take a task out of their hands and complete it himself to ensure his most exacting standards were met, then send them a copy of the finished product for their review and learning.

Over time, the team had grown tired of these inhibiting ways. Their behaviour changed: there was attention-seeking drama, non-ownership of problems, occasional sick days. CP was perplexed. From his perspective, he was supporting them heavily by rolling up his sleeves and showing them how to deliver better product and service to the business. The fact is, however, CP was stealing from them. He was stealing their potential, and they did not like it.

CP was displaying the classic fixed mindset trait of pursuit of perfection (we discuss how perfection holds us back in Chapter 9). In doing so, CP failed to recognize that people own their own potential. Whether or not a person chooses to live up to that potential is ultimately a journey for them. Whether our team members achieve their potential is not a reflection of our ability as leaders; it's a reflection of their growth mindset.

Ultimately, I supported CP in his shift towards growth mindset. CP had to learn for himself that his team's mistakes were not his failure. Whilst the way his legal team behaved contributed to his leadership brand, he had to detach his self-esteem from that brand (we discuss leadership brand in Chapter 5). He had to submerge his ego (we discuss this in Chapter 7) and allow trust to flow (we discuss this in Chapter 15). CP had to learn how to return his team's potential back into their hands as rightful owners of that potential. By encouraging CP's responsibility for cultivating his own potential for growth, we increased the probability that his team would cultivate their own potential for growth too.

When we face a choice in how to respond, we must choose the path of growth in ourselves. When people see us choosing growth, they are being led onto the path of growth too.

Decentralizing our decision-making

Under traditional leadership structures, organizations have made leadership synonymous with decision-making authority. When we assess salary bands for various levels of hierarchy in our organization, we look at objective measures such as number of line managed people and committee seats. When we design our authority manuals and governance frameworks, we determine authority based on title and position. And this authority is synonymous with power, which is held in the hands of the few who identify strongly with it. Leaders assume that because they have been given the authority, they must administer and control it themselves. Authority becomes sole authority.

In fact, there are four types of authority, set out in Table 17.1. Out of the four types, sole authority should be the exception.

Table 17.1 Types of authority and when they should be applied

Individual decision-making	Appropriate when a problem is simple or the individual with authority is the subject matter expert	Sole	Making a decision without input from others – for example, deciding bonuses for your direct reports
		Delegated	Assigning a problem to a team member who has authority to decide – for example, delegating a task to a team member who routinely does work of that nature
Collaborative decision-making	Appropriate when a problem is complex and there is no one expert and team members work well in collaborative thinking	Participative	Seeking input from team members who can influence your views (however, the ultimate decision lies with you) – for example, seeking input on departmental strategy and budget
		Consensus	Seeking input from all team members, ensuring everyone's opinions are heard, to reach a consensus view – for example, establishing a team process for applying for and taking annual leave

As leaders, we often shy away from collaborative decision-making. This is often because we assume we are 'expected' to decide or delegate. In truth, by failing to involve our team members in our thinking, ideas generation and decision-making, we are leaving money on the table. We do not have all the answers, experience, and expertise. In fact, we are further from the coal face than we often think. We rely on a small group of trusted advisors to stay connected with what is happening and rarely seek input from team members further down the reporting chain who have first hand, first sight knowledge of what is really going on. Deploying a wide variety of decision-making approaches in day-to-day decision-making transforms the experience and effectiveness of you as a leader and of your team as future leaders.

I have summarized in Table 17.2, a high-level guide in assessing when to apply each decision-making approach. The process involves us paying deliberate attention to the impact our choice will have on the people around us.

Table 17.2 Core questions to ask in selecting a decision-making approach and rationale for use

Authority type	Core question	Rationale for use
First, consider **sole** authority. See it as the exception, not the rule.	Is it imperative that I limit decision-making to me?	Sole decision-making should be used when you have enough information to make the decision yourself, the matter is confidential and really should not be shared with team members, or it could harm the team or disrupt its dynamics to involve others in the decision-making process.

If sole does not apply, consider **delegated** authority.	Is this an opportunity for a team member to learn?	You should constantly seek to use delegated decision-making for the sake of your team's learning. If you give people opportunities to learn through making decisions for themselves and experiencing the consequences of those choices, you are supporting their knowledge and experience of what great decision-making looks like in practice.
Always consider **participative** authority as an alternative.	Could this decision impact others unfavourably?	Participative decision-making is appropriate if a team member has specific expertise that you need to make the decision or when a problem could have negative impact on others. It will improve the quality of your decision-making.
There may be strong reasons that require **consensus** authority.	Is this decision fundamental to building trust and inclusion?	Consensus decision-making is appropriate if the problem is core to the team and there is no single expert. It is also appropriate if ownership by all team members is critical to success – that is, situations where if team buy-in is not built into the process of decision-making, it is unlikely that the desired outcome will be achieved.

Ultimately, as leaders, we are accountable for the decisions of our team. But, what, as leaders, are we missing out on when we elect to use individual over collaborative decision-making? The opportunity cost is high. What we lose are new ideas, perspectives, learning, creativity, innovation, experimentation, upskilling, and leadership development.

If we want to unleash the limitless potential of our team members to bring us closer to making our highest contribution, we must decentralize our decision-making and gift our teams the power of autonomy.

Less authority, more autonomy

A major barrier to decentralizing decision-making is the uncertainty around the boundaries between responsibility and accountability. When I talk to leaders about their challenges and stresses, the issue of team members not stepping up to take responsibility is a common source of complaint. From the perspective of many results-focused leaders, when a task is delegated, the team member should 'just get it done'. From the perspective of the team member, however, unless they have a mandate to step up, be creative, be explorative and use discretion when the path forward is unclear or uncertain, they do not see delegation as the transfer of responsibility.

When we make choices in what, when and how we delegate tasks, decisions, and choices, we need to become deliberate in our thinking on who has responsibility for what, and the impact this has on accountability. It is not enough to say what we want delivered and when. We need to transfer the mantle of care and concern for what might be and focus on what our team members may need by way of support in carrying that mantle.

To achieve this, first we need to be clear in our minds on the difference between accountability and responsibility. Responsibility is our ability to perform or complete assigned tasks and respond to situations and events as they arise. It is, by its nature, task focused. In the workplace, responsibility is often associated with blame, fault, or guilt which could be why team members are often resistant to taking responsibility. Accountability, on the other hand, is the recognition and acknowledgment of our responsibilities; being aware of, and answerable for, the outcomes of our actions, decisions, and mistakes. In the workplace, accountability is literally the ability or obligation to assess and report on events, tasks, and experiences. It is how a leader responds and takes ownership of the outcomes of a task. In short, the difference between accountability and responsibility is that we are responsible for things and accountable to people. Both are personal, mature, and conscious choices that come from within.

Although we often think the terms accountability and responsibility are synonymous, several characteristics separate them. I have set out in Table 17.3 the contrasting features of responsibility and accountability.

Table 17.3 The contrasting features of responsibility and accountability

Responsibility	Accountability
Obligation to perform a task or comply with a requirement	Answerability for the outcome of a task or project
Imposed by decision or structure	Accepted by will
Can be delegated	Cannot be delegated
Binary and linear obligation between team member and leader	Nonbinary and nonlinear obligation to people and organization

As leaders, we often see accountability as something we are compelled to assume when something goes wrong, and we have failed to take adequate steps to prevent it happening. So, when we delegate responsibility to our team members, our focus is on narrowing the scope for making errors, mistakes or poor judgement calls. We choose not to relinquish control; we direct how things should be done and we micromanage delivery. In short, we retain responsibility out of fear of failure or reputational damage.

In doing so we miss a valuable opportunity. We must flick the switch from protectionism to *proactive accountability*; building a culture of accountability that encourages all leaders and team members to assume control over their own outcomes. This is a shift in attention during task completion from what we need to do to avoid the task being delayed, having errors or otherwise being insufficient. In its place we choose to focus on what we can do to support the team member in assuming risk and reward.

There are steps we can take to encourage proactive accountability and responsibility:

Not brandishing people accountable

Statements like 'This one's on you!' and 'I told you so!' do not engender learning or growth; they shame people and encourage them to fear mistakes. Team members learn to accept accountability for themselves when they are given responsibility and experience consequences first hand in an environment of support and encouragement. There is no need to punish a team member for making a mistake; it is sufficient to have a discussion on the impact and consequences of the mistake and the learning that comes from that.

Being a responsible role model for accountability

We must be the example for behaviours that we want to see in our team members. When we show them what it looks like to be responsible and accountable, they feel empowered to follow suit. Think, for a moment, about how you delegate tasks and projects. Do you take time to explain the bigger picture and join the dots between successful delivery and achieving personal purpose and goals? (Refer to Chapter 14 for greater detail on how to shift from tasks to flow activities.) Similarly, there are bounteous opportunities in day-to-day work to be creative, innovative, and experimental. Role model this to team members to encourage them to use skills of discretion, judgement, and mitigating risk. We cannot expect our team to step up to growth unless we are stepping up too.

Promoting a culture of accountability

Create transparency regarding what accountability and responsibility look like in action. De-mystify standards and expectations by explaining how a team member should and should not act and the parameters of authority and decision-making. Develop, with your team's input, a team promise or protocol that documents the behaviours that are consistent with expected standards. Develop team policies, procedures and processes that document the 'how' and 'why', so team members know what choices to make when the path forward is uncertain. The test is this: if you are hit by a bus tomorrow, can your team members make good choices without you being there to tell them what to do?

Reporting increases accountability and responsibility

Lifting the lid on what is happening as opposed to what people are saying is happening is a sure-footed path to greater accountability and responsibility. When we regularly report on and celebrate milestone achievements, small wins, and progress in the face of adversity, team members are motivated to do more. Receiving praise and gratitude for efforts and being given the opportunity to unite with colleagues in success consolidates learning. It connects the dots for team members between the effort and the benefits from stretching to higher levels of responsibility and challenging ourselves beyond expectations.

Providing encouragement and support

Growth cannot happen in a vacuum, and we have a heightening responsibility to support when we want our team members to be proactively accountable. This means having regular coaching sessions to ask how team members are doing, exploring new challenges and helping them to think through the problems and hurdles they face. These sessions give us the opportunity to provide additional support if course correction is required and to give praise and encouragement to motivate team members to keep stretching.

When, as leaders, we have created an empowered culture of accountability, our teams and organizations will benefit from:

- better, faster decisions;
- greater engagement and motivation;
- increased productivity;
- greater understanding of the business and its needs;
- better delivery; and
- greater creativity and innovation.

When we encourage autonomy in our team members, we empower them to operate at their optimum potential within the parameters of their authority. When we empower them in this way, they will not live up to our expectations; they will far exceed them.

Making succession our success

When I consider the mindset of the senior leaders who have contributed to my growth and those of leaders who have not, I realize that the fundamental difference is down to one core fear: the fear of losing their positions at the top. The leader who feels the constant need to compete with their senior leadership team is ultimately trapped in the belief that their potential is limited to where they have reached and that no further success is possible. They have let fixed mindset overcome them.

Even growth leaders can have trouble letting go. They can retain responsibility for a task, not because of organizational need, but due to being overprotective. Sometimes, they attend a meeting not to contribute to better thinking in the room, but to remind others of their ultimate authority to decide. Often, they are first to arrive at the office and last to leave, not because work demands dictate it but because they want to demonstrate their unending commitment to working hard. But if we are completely honest as to why we hold onto doing leadership, it is because we are uncomfortable with the space it creates when we stop doing. The space leaves an empty void that others can step into. There is something deeply dissatisfying about allowing others to catch up with us.

Growth leaders have, however, made a deliberate decision to step up to Level 4 leadership (people development) (Maxwell, 2013). They have stepped up to a higher level of responsibility to create an optimum environment for their high potentials to become Level 4 leaders themselves in the future (we discuss creation of optimum environment for growth and learning in Chapter 13). When we accept that our ultimate role as leaders is to serve the people around us, it becomes less about if and more about when others around us will accede to higher positions, including our own positions. Our leadership in the present becomes about planning for our future and knowing when it is the right time for our team members to evolve into their highest potential.

The leader who feels that their greatest success is preparing their successor for future success is already unleashing their own highest potential.

Creating change leaders of the future is a journey into proactive accountability. We must put in place pulls and levers that ensure the people around us are fully mandated and motivated to explore and develop their potential. We let go of our attachment to authority in favour of their autonomy. We also detach from control of decision-making to make space for their ability to exercise sound judgement through increasing discretion. Above all, it means accepting that creating change leaders around us means that at some point in the future, we are empowering them to succeed us.

When I look back at my leadership career and the decisions I have made, I can say, hand on heart, that my biggest successes have been when I had evolved to the point where future leaders have succeeded me.

Our effectiveness as leaders depends on how we trust. When we believe in ourselves and our ability to grow as leaders, we role model growth leadership to those around us. We courageously let go to enable our team members to lead themselves through change and become change leaders of the future. Their success makes us rise.

When lawyers choose to lead consciously, they are advancing the future of law.

LEAP IV in a nutshell

- If people around us do not trust us, our overall effectiveness as leaders shrinks. To build trust in the workplace, we must humanize. We must pay constant attention to converting our own potential into actual growth in ourselves and those around us.
- We do this by focusing on how to improve the process of learning itself.
- We capitalize on the knowledge that exists at all levels of an organization by seeking collaborative contribution of all the people around us, regardless of hierarchy or convention. We harness the power of collective wisdom.
- By showing our own willingness to shift from fixed mindset to growth mindset, we connect people around us to their own capacity to lead themselves through this change.
- We transfer ownership of potential back into the hands of our team members so that they can be leaders of change for the future.
- First, we decentralize our decision-making. By deploying a variety of decision-making approaches – individual and collaborative – we empower our team members to take ownership of their leadership potential. In doing so, we open the gateways to new ideas, perspectives, learning, creativity, innovation, and experimentation.

- Second, we gift our team members the power of autonomy. We create a culture of accountability that encourages everyone to assume control over their own outcomes.
- If we want to unleash the limitless potential of our team members to bring us closer to making our own highest contribution, we must let them be change leaders of the future.
- Our biggest success as leaders will be when we have evolved to the point where our future leaders have succeeded us.

Chapter 18
Drawing this together

With increasing pressure from technological disruption, rising global challenges, and generational shifts in the workplace, lawyers must consciously choose to lead through change in the legal sector.

There are two keys ways in which lawyers must change; they must:

- *be more client-centric* – to respond to the demand for new business models, fit-for-purpose innovative solutions to client problems, and flexible resourcing capabilities; and
- *be more human* – to motivate the new generation of lawyers and harness the unlimited potential of the technological future of law.

This requires lawyers to radically change the way they lead. They must become conscious lawyers.

It takes four leaps to courageously lead high-performance teams into the future of law.

Leap I: *Connect* to the leader in you

We must connect to who we are as leaders, not who we tell ourselves we are. This means letting go of ego and showing the world who we are from the inside out.

Leap II: *Awaken* your purpose

We must shift from focusing on what we have achieved to focusing on our limitless potential for having greater impact. This means stepping up to a higher level of integrity as leaders. This involves role modelling the shift from fixed mindset to growth mindset and using flow to transform our leadership.

Leap III: *Relate* to the people around you

We must lead change by shifting focus from achieving high performance results to unleashing unlimited potential in the people around us. This means shifting our focus from results to people, and choosing purpose over profits. By transforming people's experience of performance as learning, we empower them to convert their potential to achievement through their efforts. In this way, change flows.

Leap IV: *Entrust* others to fulfil their potential

We must commit to developing our people to be courageous change leaders of the future. This means trusting ourselves enough to let go of authority. We must grant our people autonomy to follow their own journeys of learning and growth on their paths to fulfilling their highest potential.

When we have the courage to CARE, we are the future of law.

Epilogue

It is April 2018, eight weeks after my ski accident, and I am sitting on my couch with my 6-year-old son by my side. He looks at the three-inch scar on my right leg and asks, 'Is it sore, Mummy?' 'I don't know, Darling', I reply. At this point, I am not able to touch my scar to know how it feels. The permanent mark where the surgeon's incision was made is too painful a reminder of the events of the accident, the harm felt, and the rehabilitative journey of surgery, physiotherapy and emotional care. 'But it's cool, Mummy,' he says, 'bet no one else has a scar as awesome as that.'

This exchange of words was a turning point for me. I realized then that my journey had only begun. It took many more months to discover what I needed to learn on my path of transformation. Whilst I had been practising submerging my ego for some time, I had not fully appreciated, until then, my complete intolerance of imperfection. I started to unmask the reasons for my inability to admit pain and the impact this had on my capacity to feel joy in the moment. I discovered that I had become so brittle, unforgiving and resentful of myself and others that I had literally snapped at the knee.

In continuing on the path of recovery, I learnt how to be more flexible, forgiving, and compassionate for others, but mostly for myself. I learnt that by opening my heart to myself through self-care, I was able to embrace myself fully and completely, even the parts I did not like. I started to see that there is beauty in every scar. And that it is the scars that make us wonderfully unique in who we are. This learning gave me courage to start touching my scar, consciously examining the lessons that were there for me in the accident. Until, finally, I was able to accept the amazing beauty of my scar in all its imperfection.

Today, when I touch my scar, I feel love in my heart. I can admire it, caress it, and soothe myself from it. When I spend moments admiring how it looks, I say: 'Thank you for the learning. It is truly a gift, from which I have become who I really am.'

We all have a journey to take in life. Our experiences mould us into who we are. Some experiences bring us joy and fulfilment – we achieve results, gain rewards, and are recognized for our efforts. These build our self-esteem and sense of worth. Other experiences harm us – we are betrayed, wounded, or excluded. What happens in our past can limit our future. But the choice of impact is ours. When we subscribe to the guiding belief that we all have a greater calling, we are lifted in our aspirations of what that will be. We can make our highest contributions in life and work if we simply dedicate ourselves to that calling every day.

Experiences have taught me that when we have the courage to choose the path of learning through life, unlimited opportunities flow. It starts with one step, a choice to live life consciously.

Acknowledgements

Writing *The Conscious Lawyer* has been an experience of immeasurable joy. I am at my deepest level of fulfilment when I am in the process of writing. But I cannot take sole credit for *The Conscious Lawyer*. It is the product of the vast army of teachers, role models, mentors, coaches, and supporters that have surrounded me my whole life.

First, and always foremost, I thank Paul, my best friend. It is not easy being married to Kiran Scarr, I know, but your belief in me is unconditional and unending. I would not be where I am now if it were not for you. Also, I give deep gratitude to Isobel and Oliver, my teachers in life. Not one day goes by without me being thankful that you chose me to be your mum in this life.

To my wider family, I thank you too, with an open heart. Mum and Dad, I thank you, particularly, for shining the light of living life in service to others. Janet and Pete, I thank you for loving me unconditionally as a daughter from the first day we met.

Thank you, also, to my soul tribe of inspirational women who have showered me with guidance and love on this journey to greater consciousness – particularly, Rawan Albina, Helen Williams, Laura Carr, Joanna Dawson, and Iris Van der Veken. Thank you to my many colleagues, clients, and friends over the years, without whom I would not have learnt what I know. Special mention here to the courageous women of conscious supper club and book club; we all have our struggles and strife but, above all, we love one another.

To Alison Jones and the amazing team at Practical Inspiration Publishing. Thank you for your belief and support in getting us here.

And, finally, I want to thank Mrs Grewar, my sixth-form English teacher, who told me: 'It does not matter what you go on to do in life, Kiran. You will always be a girl who can make a difference with her words.'

Bibliography

Academy of Management Insights, *15 signs you work with a narcissist, Machiavellian or psychopath* (no date). Available from: https://journals. aom.org/doi/full/10.5465/amp.2017.0005.summary

Ade, Y., *7 subtle signs which show that you have an ego problem*, Medium (2021, 15 May). Available from: https://medium.com/illumination/7-subtle-signs-which-show-that-you-have-an-ego-problem-f2bf582e1005

Beisser, A., *The paradoxical theory of change*, The Gestalt Therapy (no date). Available from: www.gestalt.org/arnie.htm

Benson, K., *The anger iceberg*, The Gottman Institute (no date). Available from: www.gottman.com/blog/the-anger-iceberg/

Botsman, R., *Who can you trust? How technology brought us together and why it might drive us apart* (2018) Public Affairs.

Brassey, J., Coe, E., Dewhurst, M., Enomoto, K., Jeffrey, B., Giarola, R., and Herbig, B., *Addressing employee burnout: Are you solving the right problem?* McKinsey Health Institute (2022, 27 May). Available from: www.mckinsey.com/mhi/our-insights/addressing-employee-burnout-are-you-solving-the-right-problem

Catalino, N. and Marnane, K., *When women lead, workplaces should listen*, McKinsey Quarterly (2019, 11 December). Available from: www.mckinsey.com/featured-insights/leadership/when-women-lead-workplaces-should-listen

Chamorro-Premuzic, T., *Why do so many incompetent men become leaders? (And how to fix it)* (2019) Harvard Business Review Press.

Covey, S. The 7 habits of highly effective people, 30th anniversary edition (2020) Simon & Schuster.

Crossroad Advantage, *Negative reality norm theory or what's wrong with happy endings* (no date). Available from: www.crossroadadvantage. com/single-post/2018/11/26/negative-reality-norm-theory-or-whats-wrong-with-happy-endings

Csikszentmihalyi, M., *Flow: The psychology of optimal experience*, Modern Classics edition (2008) Harper Perennial.

Deloitte Australia and Victorian Equal Opportunity and Human Rights Commission, *Waiter, is that inclusion in my soup? A new recipe to improve business performance* (2013). Available from: www2.deloitte.com/content/dam/Deloitte/au/Documents/human-capital/deloitte-au-hc-diversity-inclusion-soup-0513.pdf

Dutton, K., *The wisdom of psychopaths: Lessons in life from saints, spies and serial killers* (2013) Arrow Books.

Dwek, C., *Mindset: Changing the way you think to fulfil your potential,* updated edition (2017) Robinson.

Erikson, T., *Surrounded by idiots: The four types of human behaviour (or, how to understand those who cannot be understood)* (2019) Vermilion.

Espinoza, C., Ukleja, M., and Rusch, C., *Managing the Millennials: Discover the core competencies for managing today's workforce,* 2nd edition (2010) John Wiley & Sons Ltd.

Forster, E.M., *A room with a view* (1995) Dover Publications.

Gallwey, W.T., *The inner game of work: Focus, learning, pleasure, and mobility in the workplace* (2001) Random House Trade.

García, H. and Miralles, F., *Ikigai: The Japanese secret to a long and happy life* (2017) Penguin Life.

Gardner, W.L., Cogliser, C.C., Davis, K.M., and Dickens, M.P., 'Authentic leadership: A review of the literature and research agenda' in *The Leadership Quarterly*, 22 (6), 1120–1145 (2011).

GBS Corporate Training, *The cost of poor leadership on your revenue and culture* (2017, 13 July). Available from: www.gbscorporate.com/blog/the-cost-of-poor-leadership-on-your-revenue-and-culture

Gratton, L. and Scott, A., *The 100-year life: Living and working in an age of longevity,* 2nd edition (2020) Bloomsbury.

Greentarget, *2017 predictive legal trends* (2017). Available from: https://greentarget.com/wp-content/uploads/2017/03/2017-Legal-Outlook-Final-Greentarget.pdf

Hay, L., *You can heal your life* (1984) Hay House.

Hendricks, G., *The big leap: Conquer your hidden fear and take life to the next level* (2009) Harper Collins.

Holiday, R., *Ego is the enemy: The fight to master our greatest opponent* (2017) Profile Books.

Hoomans, J., *35,000 decisions: The great choices of strategic leaders*, Leading Edge (2015, 20 March). Available from: https://go.roberts.edu/leadingedge/the-great-choices-of-strategic-leaders

Kline, N., *Time to think: Listening to ignite the human mind* (2002) Cassell Illustrated.

Kotter, J., *Leading change*, illustrated edition (2012) Harvard Business Review Press.

Lexis Nexis, *Lead or follow? How law firms adapt to a changing market* (2021). Available from: www.lexisnexis.co.uk/research-and-reports/lead-or-follow-how-law-firms-adapt-to-a-changing-market.html

Luft, J. and Ingham, H., 'The Johari window, a graphic model of interpersonal awareness' in *Proceedings of the Western Training Laboratory in Group Development* (1955) University of California, Los Angeles.

Mackey, J., McIntosh, S., and Phipps, C., *Conscious leadership: Elevating humanity through business* (2020) Portfolio Penguin.

Maslow, A., 'A theory of human motivation' in *Psychological Review*, 50 (4), 370–396 (1943).

Maxwell, J., *The 5 levels of leadership: Proven steps to maximise your potential* (2013) Center Street.

McKeown, G., *The essentialist: The disciplined pursuit of less* (2014) Penguin Random House.

Perls, F., 'Four lectures' in J. Fagan and I.L. Shepherd (eds), *Gestalt therapy now: Theory techniques, applications* (1970) The Gestalt Journal Press, pp. 14–38.

Ranadive, A., *Why 'ego is the enemy' and what we can do about it*, Medium (2017, 17 July). Available from: https://medium.com/@ameet/why-ego-is-the-enemy-and-what-we-can-do-about-it-a4eae45a81d8#:~:text=One%20of%20the%20biggest%20reasons,required%20to%20achieve%20your%20goals

Reina, D. and Reina, M., *Trust and betrayal in the workplace: Building effective relationships in your organization* (1999) Berrett-Koehler.

Senge, P., *The fifth discipline: The art and practice of the learning organisation*, 2nd edition (2006) Random House.

Solicitors Regulation Authority, *How diverse is the solicitors' profession?* (2022, 29 April). Available from: www.sra.org.uk/sra/equality-diversity/diversity-profession/diverse-legal-profession/

Suzuki, N., *Wabi sabi: The wisdom of imperfection* (2021) Tuttle.

The Holy Bible: Matthew 6:28, Consider the lilies.

Thomson Reuters, *What's keeping legal leaders up at night in MENA?* (2022). Available from: https://mena.thomsonreuters.com/en/resources/legal/whitepapers/2021/whats-keeping-legal-leaders-up-at-night.html

Thomson Reuters Institute, *2020 law firm business leaders report: Outlook for US-based local & regional law firms* (2020). Available from: https://legal.thomsonreuters.com/en/insights/reports/2020-law-firm-business-leaders-report

Thomson Reuters Institute, *2021 state of corporate law departments. The global COVID-19 pandemic: a catalyst for accelerating the change agenda* (2021). Available from: www.acc.com/sites/default/files/resources/upload/2021-state-of-corporate-law-departments.pdf

Tillay, M., *Which law firms have the most female equity partners?* LawCom (2021). Available from: www.law.com/international-edition/2021/07/13/which-law-firms-have-the-most-female-equity-partners/

Tolle, E., *The power of now: A guide to spiritual enlightenment* (2004) New World Library.

Tolle, E., *The new earth: create a better life* (2016) Penguin Books.

Williamson, M., *A return to love: Reflections on the principles of 'A course in miracles'* (1996) HarperOne.

Wittebrood, J., *Differences between Gen Z and Millennials*, blackbear (2021, 11 August). Available from: https://blog.blackbear.global/differences-between-gen-z-and-millennials

World Economic Forum, *The future of jobs report 2020* (2020). Available from:www.weforum.org/reports/the-future-of-jobs-report-2020/?DAG=3&gclid=CjwKCAiAjs2bBhACEiwALTBWZVOLK0iwyKFEfKp1-24crmuZWzW2BNOOOGOh0IluMocdmOSarVYGbBoCUeQQAvD_BwE

Zenger, J. and Folkman, J., *The 3 elements of trust*, Harvard Business Review (2019, 5 February). Available from: https://hbr.org/2019/02/the-3-elements-of-trust

Index

quality of life 118–119

R

responsibility 213–217
   and accountability, difference between
      213–215
   contrasting features of 214
   reporting in 217
results
   and abundance 98–99
   and competition 95–98
   detaching from 102–103
   focusing on 170, 213
   past, limitations of 99–102
   versus people 154–156

S

scarcity mindset 96, 97–98, 123
security, need of 46
Self 1 135, 136–137
Self 2 131, 136–137
self-care 83–84, 125
self-disclosure 87
self-limiting beliefs 109–110, 123
self-promotion 8
self-trust 188–189, 194–195
self-validation 183
shadow boards 198
skills gap 18
SMART goals 170
spiritual centres 75–77
strategic thinking 157
strength 124, 158
stress and boredom, balance between
      131–132
success
   optimum environment for 219–220
   and results 108

T

tangible brand value 57
tangible motivations 132
task-orientated approach 123
transactional trust 187
transformation process 120–128
   achievement recognition 124
   conscious-self 126
   courage 124

experience of now 123
external opinions 125–126
failure, acceptance of 126–128
path to fulfilment, focusing on 120–121
potentiality 123
self-care 125
troops 2
trust 163
   characteristics of 187
   circle of 186
   core elements of 185
   and fixed mindset 183–185
   and growth mindset 192–194
   importance of 185–186
   loss of 60
   in others 194, 224
   in workplace 186–188
trust tree 187–188
   compassion, value of 190–191
   empathy, value of 190
   foundation of 188–189
   potential, attention to 191–192

U

uncertainty 102–103
unknown self 87

V

values-based leadership 63–65, 127,
      151–152, 162
   personal values in workplaces 65–66
   problems in 65
   and values-deficit leadership, differences
      between 67
   values gap 65
   values in action 69–70
vocation 119–120

W

wabi sabi philosophy 82
war rooms 2
who we are, components of 59–62
women leadership behaviour 23–24
work activities/games 172
work family culture 20

Z

zone of genius 100